HAUNTED ROADS

WHERE EVERY TURN REVEALS A GHOSTLY LEGEND.

EVE S EVANS

Copyright © 2025 by Eve S Evans

No part of this book may be reproduced, distributed, or transmitted in any form or by any means, including photocopying, recording, or other electronic or mechanical methods, without the prior written permission of the publisher, except in the case of brief quotations embodied in critical reviews and certain other noncommercial uses permitted by copyright law.

This book is a work of nonfiction. While every effort has been made to ensure the accuracy of the information presented, the author and publisher assume no responsibility for errors or omissions. The events and characters portrayed in this book are based on factual accounts and real-life individuals, but names and certain identifying details may have been changed or fictionalized to protect privacy.

Cover Design: Eve S Evans
Interior Design: Eve S Evans

First Edition: March 2025

Eve invites readers to subscribe to her email newsletter, where she conducts several "mystery box" giveaways each year. The link to subscribe can also be found in her Instagram bio: eves.evansauthor.

Newsletter Signup (mailchi.mp)

The giveaways feature a variety of items, including bookmarks, autographed paperbacks, merchandise for book lovers, horror-themed items, paranormal merchandise, and much more. Additionally, readers can explore autographed spooky book bundles available in her TikTok shop.

https://www.tiktok.com/@author_eve_evans

To my beloved mom,

It's been ten years since you became an angel, yet your love continues to guide me every day. Your strength, kindness, and wisdom remain etched in my heart. This book is dedicated to you, a tribute to the countless ways you've inspired me. Thank you for being my eternal source of love and light. This one is for you.

ROADSIDE MYSTERY

CHAPTER 1

ROADSIDE MYSTERY

A real ghostly encounter

Ten years ago... It's almost surprising to me that it has been that long since that night. It's funny how time works; there are events in your life that no matter how many revolutions the clock makes, they cling to you like shadows, refusing to fade. That's how I felt as I drove home, the dark road stretching endlessly before me, illuminated only by the headlights of my aging sedan. I thought my life had changed forever that night. In a way, it did, just not in the way I originally envisioned.

Anna was a country girl, and I knew it well when I

married her. With her sun-kissed hair and laughter that echoed like a stream, she was everything I admired. Me? I was a city boy, comfortable in a metropolis buzzing with more than a million souls. Still, I couldn't ignore her dreams of raising our family on a sprawling ranch, surrounded by horses just like she had in her childhood. The thought of it turned my stomach, but my sole purpose in life, from the moment I first laid eyes on her, was to make that woman smile. "If you want a ranch, then a ranch it is," I had told her, swallowing my fears.

I made my living as an accountant, steadily climbing the ranks at a reputable firm. Giving all that up for a life in the country felt daunting, but to my surprise, they allowed me to work remotely, balancing video calls with trips back to the office.

These trips were a double-edged sword. On one hand, I could revisit the city and indulge in my favorite haunts—like that little diner with the best pancakes or the bookstore where I lost countless afternoons. On the other hand, it meant long, exhausting drives that forced me out of bed before dawn and returned me well after dark. Anna used to wait up for me, her eyes bright with love, but soon it became routine, and we both agreed it wasn't necessary for her to stay awake.

I glanced at the dashboard clock, feeling the weight of fatigue pulling at my eyelids. I was about an hour from home, and I could already feel the effects of the drive. The window was down, despite the chilling air just above freezing, and the music blared—a rock anthem that might have made even a rowdy group of teens shake their heads in disapproval.

"Come on, stay awake, just a little longer," I muttered to myself, gripping the steering wheel tighter. The idea of pulling over for a quick nap flitted through my mind, but the thought of not being next to Anna in bed kept me from doing so. I could picture her there, the soft glow of the bedside lamp illuminating her peaceful face. "You're just being overcautious," I reassured myself, but as the road stretched on, doubt crept in.

I squinted against the darkness, willing my eyes to stay open. A quick glance at my phone revealed a missed call from Anna. My heart twinged. "Hey, babe, just checking in," she had likely said. I should have called her back, but the thought of her voice, warm and inviting, made my resolve waver. I couldn't let fatigue win. I was committed now; I just needed to push through.

"Just a few more miles, and you'll be home," I whispered, and with that, I turned up the volume, hoping the music would fuel my determination.

Another fifteen minutes slipped by as I fought against the heavy pull of exhaustion. My eyelids felt as if they were stitched shut, and even the rhythmic hum of the tires on asphalt couldn't rouse me from the impending darkness that loomed in my mind. I glanced at the clock on the dashboard; it was well past midnight, and I was still miles from home. I could feel the fatigue settling deep in my bones, a weariness that clawed at my consciousness.

"I can't keep this up," I muttered to myself, my voice barely breaking the silence of the car. The sound echoed back at me, a reminder of my solitude on that desolate stretch of highway. I pulled over to the side of the road, the tires crunching on gravel, and took a deep breath, welcoming the chill of the night air that seeped in when I opened the door.

Stepping out, I felt the cool breeze wrapping around me, invigorating yet unsettling. My legs protested with stiffness, a reminder of the long hours spent hunched behind the wheel, navigating the dark, lonely road. I paced back and forth for a few minutes, shoving my hands into my pockets and kicking small pebbles along the shoulder. "Just a quick break," I whispered to myself, hoping the movement would spark some energy. "You can do this."

The stars twinkled above, indifferent to my plight, and I took a moment to collect my thoughts. "What would Anna say if she were here?" I wondered, imagining her voice, always so calming and rational. "You need to rest. Be smart." But I was stubborn, unwilling to admit that my body was signaling for a reprieve.

After a few minutes of wandering, I climbed back into the car, feeling a touch more alert. I turned the ignition, and the engine roared to life, vibrating with a familiar hum that felt reassuring. The rhythmic thrum of the tires against the pavement steadied me, and I thought, maybe I could make it home without drifting off. I reached down for my soda; a quick jolt of caffeine was what I needed.

But when I looked down, my heart sank. The cup was empty. "Great," I groaned, frustration bubbling up. I should have stopped for a refill somewhere along the way. I cursed under my breath, but the irritation quickly faded as I returned my gaze to the road.

That's when it happened. A figure appeared almost out of nowhere, directly in my path. Time slowed as I realized what was happening, my mind reeling. "No, no, no!" I shouted, but it was too late. Even with superhuman reflexes, there was no way to avoid him. My foot slammed down on the brake, but the impact was already inevitable.

The moment of collision felt surreal, a jarring shock that reverberated through the car. I couldn't even process it as the man seemed to vanish, either over the hood or off to the side. It was a blur, a haunting ghost of a moment that left my heart racing and my mind spiraling.

As I sat there, breathless and frozen, a whirlwind of thoughts crashed over me. "What just happened? Did I just…" I gripped the steering wheel so tightly my knuckles turned white. The weight of reality settled heavily on my chest. I had just undoubtedly killed a man, and the consequences of my actions loomed large and terrifying in my mind.

"What was he doing there?" I tried to rationalize, but deep down, I knew the truth. If I had been paying attention, if I hadn't let fatigue cloud my judgment, this wouldn't have happened. "God, I should have seen him," I whispered, my voice trembling.

With shaking hands, I turned off the engine and sat in the heavy silence of the night, listening to the faint rustle of leaves and the distant echo of my own heartbeat. The car's metal frame clicked and popped as it cooled, a stark contrast to the chaos swirling in my mind. I stepped out into the cold night air, unsure of what I would find.

As I took a tentative step toward the road, my phone buzzed in my pocket, a reminder of the world I was about to step away from. I hesitated, my thoughts racing. Should I call Anna? But what would I even say? I pulled out my phone, staring at the screen, caught between the urge to reach out to her and my desperate need to understand the gravity of the situation first. I needed to know what had happened before dragging her into this nightmare.

I walked down the center of the road, my sneakers crunching against the gravel beneath me. The cool night air wrapped around me like a thin blanket, but my heart raced, pounding in my chest as I scanned both sides of the road for any sign of the man. I took each step slowly, deliberately, my eyes darting between the shadows cast by the dim streetlights.

The echoes of my footsteps felt unnaturally loud, amplifying my anxiety as I ventured further than I intended—at least twice the distance I thought he could have traveled. But there was nothing. No sign of him. My stomach twisted tighter with each futile glance, and panic began to creep in, gnawing at the edges of my mind.

"Think, think, think," I muttered to myself, almost pleadingly. Should I have called 911? The thought flickered through my mind like an old film reel but faded just as quickly, drowned out by the thudding of my heart.

I retraced my steps back to my car, the familiar sight of it somehow grounding me, yet filled with dread. I stood in front of the vehicle, peering closely at the hood and bumper, desperately searching for any indication that I had indeed hit him. My breath hitched as I examined the surface, hoping for some sign—any sign—that he had been there. But the front of my car looked pristine, unblemished, as if it had never touched another soul.

"What the hell..." I whispered, my voice a shaky breath that hung in the air. I ran my fingers over the smooth surface, searching for hidden dents or scratches, but there was nothing. Hitting someone should have left a mark, right? I felt a wave of confusion wash over me, mingling with my rising dread.

I felt my hands instinctively rise to my head, fingers tangling in my hair as I tried to process what was happening. "No sign of a wreck, and I can't find him... does that mean it's okay for me to leave?" The thought flickered through my mind, but it felt wrong, like I was trying to convince myself of something I didn't believe.

Just then, I heard it—a crunch of gravel behind me, soft but distinct. My body tensed, and I turned around, the motion feeling surreal, like I was moving through molasses.

What met my eyes sent a shiver down my spine. The man I had seen earlier stood there, his face pale as moonlight, an eerie stillness surrounding him. I felt a chill race up my spine, but I was also oddly relieved to see him standing there, alive—or so I thought.

"Hey! Are you okay?" I called out, my voice wavering as I took a cautious step forward.

He didn't respond, his gaze locked onto mine with

an intensity that made my skin crawl. And then, just like that, he seemed to flicker, his form wavering as if he were made of smoke before my very eyes. In an instant, he vanished, leaving only the echo of my heartbeat and the rustle of the night air behind.

For a moment, I stood frozen, my mind racing. First, I was terrified of the possibility of having harmed someone; now, I was gripped by an entirely different kind of fear. What had just happened? If you asked me which was worse at that moment—being arrested for hitting a man or witnessing the impossible—I wouldn't have known how to answer.

Desperation clawed at me, and I did the only thing that felt right. I called Anna.

When she picked up, her sleepy voice was thick with confusion. "Hello? Who is this?"

"It's me, Anna," I stammered, my words tumbling out in a jumbled mess. "I think... I think I just hit someone with my car. But he's... he's gone. I don't know what to do!"

Her voice sharpened, concern cutting through the haze of sleep. "Slow down! What happened?"

I took a shaky breath, trying to gather my thoughts as I recounted the nightmarish events. It took ten agonizing minutes for me to spill the entire story, my words tumbling out in a frantic rush. "I swear, I saw him right in front of me, and then he just—he vanished!"

Anna was silent for a moment, the weight of my words hanging in the air. "Are you sure you're okay? You sound freaked out."

"I don't even know if I'm okay! I might have killed someone... or I might be losing my mind!"

"Just get home," she said finally, her voice steadying me slightly. "We'll talk about it when you're here. Please, just drive carefully."

I ended the call, staring into the darkness that surrounded me, feeling utterly lost.
That is exactly what I do the moment I walk in the door—haggard, exhausted, and feeling like I'm losing my mind. The air feels thick, almost suffocating, as I close the door behind me, shutting out the world. My heart races, a relentless drumbeat that echoes in my ears. I'm not sure I did a good job describing what happened that night on the road to

her. I probably sounded like a deranged, sleep-deprived buffoon, but I was shaken.

"Are you sure you're okay?" my wife had asked, her brow furrowing with concern as I relayed my story. I could still hear her voice echoing in my mind, a mix of disbelief and worry. "You didn't imagine it, did you?"

"No, I swear," I replied, my voice trembling. "I saw him—right there in the headlights. A pale figure, drifting like mist."

Since that night, I've done research about the area, discovering that I'm not the only one who has claimed to see a spirit wandering those dark stretches. Reports stretch back decades, each one echoing my own experience. The stories are chilling, filled with descriptions of a man in white who appears at twilight, his face a mask of sorrow. But knowing I'm not alone doesn't offer any solace. I can't help but wonder: Why do some spirits linger while others seem to move on? Are any truly able to escape the tether of this world? I shudder at the thought, a deep chill coursing down my spine whenever I think of the paranormal and what lies beyond. Each question swirls in my mind like leaves caught in an autumn wind, and I can't shake the feeling that even if I find answers, they'll only lead to more uncertainty. What if the spirit I saw was begging for help, trapped in a cycle he couldn't break? The thought sends a fresh wave of unease coursing through me, reminding me that sometimes, it's better to leave certain mysteries unsolved. I glance at my wife, her expression a mix of concern and confusion, and I realize she bears the weight of my fears too. It's a burden I wish I could lift from both our shoulders.

Ten years later, the memory clings to me like fog on a chilly morning, wrapping around me until I can hardly breathe. I always thought time would wash it away like rain on pavement, but instead, it has become more vivid, more haunting. Every time I drive that road, a shiver of dread tightens my grip on the steering wheel. My heart quickens as shadows dance along the asphalt, whispering secrets I dare not confront.

"I swear I saw something!" I remember shouting into the void of the night, desperate for validation. But the only answer is the whisper of the wind, sending chills down my spine. I recall the night I thought I killed someone, only to encounter a ghost instead. The specter still haunts my dreams. Each glance in the rearview mirror feels like a reminder that some things, once seen, can never be unseen.

THE PHANTOM OF LOGAN COUNTY

CHAPTER 2

THE PHANTOM OF LOGAN COUNTY

As the sun dips below the horizon, casting long shadows over the winding curves of 22 Mine Road, an unsettling chill sweeps through the air, wrapping itself around the trees like a shroud. The road, nestled in the heart of Logan County, West Virginia, is less a mere stretch of asphalt and more a portal to the spectral realms, where the ghost of Mamie Thurman plays tricks on unsuspecting drivers. This chilling tale begins in the summer of 1932, a year that would etch itself into local lore, forever intertwining the fate of a vibrant woman with the shadows of a darkened road.

Mamie Morrison, born on September 12, 1900, in a quaint, sun-dappled town nestled in the rolling hills of Kentucky, was a woman whose presence radiated charm and charisma. With her warm, inviting smile that could light up the gloomiest of days and a quick wit that kept conversations lively, she effortlessly captivated everyone who crossed her path. Her laughter, melodic and infectious, echoed through the narrow streets of her hometown, drawing people in like moths to a flame. Mamie was not just a fixture of her community; she was its heartbeat, a vibrant embodiment of the spirit of the roaring twenties.

In 1924, Mamie and her husband, Jack Thurman, a dedicated patrolman with a strong sense of duty, made the move to Logan County. Jack, with his rugged good looks and unwavering commitment to law and order, believed he had achieved the picture-perfect life. Their modest home, adorned with blooming flower boxes and a white picket fence, seemed to symbolize their ideal existence. However, beneath Mamie's saintly facade lay whispers of a tumultuous personal life, a stark contrast to the idyllic image she projected. As Jack patrolled the streets of Logan County each night, ensuring the safety of its residents, Mamie found herself drawn into the vibrant nightlife that pulsed through the town.

Under the cover of darkness, Mamie transformed from devoted wife to the life of the party, frequenting local clubs and speakeasies where the air was thick with jazz and the clinking of glasses. She was known for her vivacious nature and friendly disposition, easily mingling with patrons and making friends wherever she went. The dimly lit rooms, filled with smoke and laughter, became her sanctuary, a place where she could shed the constraints of her daily life and embrace the exhilarating freedom that came with dancing and revelry. Her captivating presence turned heads, and as she twirled in her flapper dresses, adorned with sequins that sparkled under the low light, it was as if the world revolved around her.

However, as summer blossomed that year, so did the tension surrounding her personal life. Whispers began to swirl like autumn leaves caught in a gust of wind, suggesting that Mamie was involved with several prominent men in the area. Among them was Harry Robertson, a suave local banker who lived nearby. Harry, with his charming smile and sharp suits, was known for his affluence and influence in the community. The rumors of their clandestine meetings sent ripples through Logan County, igniting a firestorm of jealousy and speculation. Mamie's flirtatious nature, once considered endearing, now became a source of intrigue and scandal.

As the days grew longer and the sultry summer nights unfolded, the intricate web of jealousy, deceit, and betrayal began to tighten around Mamie. Friends turned into foes, and once-loyal confidants whispered behind closed doors, fueling the flames of gossip that threatened to consume her. The very essence of her lively spirit, which had once been a source of joy, now became a target for those who felt betrayed by her actions. Jack, dedicated and oblivious to the turmoil brewing in his wife's life, continued to walk the streets with a sense of pride, unaware that his picture-perfect world was crumbling around him.

Mamie, caught in the crossfire of her own desires and the expectations of society, found herself teetering on the edge of a precipice. The vibrant nightlife that had once exhilarated her now felt like a double-edged sword, promising both ecstasy and despair. The thrill of dancing and laughter mingled with the gnawing anxiety of being discovered, creating an internal battle that raged within her. The summer sun began to set on her seemingly perfect life, casting long shadows that hinted at the tragic fate that awaited her. The stage was set for a dramatic climax, one that would forever alter the lives of those involved and leave an indelible mark on the fabric of the community.

On the fateful evening of June 21, 1932, the tranquil atmosphere of Logan County was irrevocably shattered. The sun was dipping below the horizon, casting long shadows over the dense thicket of blackberries that bordered 22 Mine Road. It was in this seemingly serene setting that young Bobby Thompson, a local boy with a penchant for foraging, stumbled upon a sight that would haunt him for the rest of his life. As he pushed through the brambles, his fingers brushing against the ripe, glistening berries, he caught a glimpse of something that sent his heart racing—a lifeless figure sprawled amid the underbrush.

The moment he recognized the pale, delicate features of Mamie Thurman, the weight of the world seemed to collapse around him. Her body lay eerily still, a stark contrast to the vibrant, wild foliage surrounding her. Mamie's throat had been brutally slashed from ear to ear, the grotesque gash a gruesome testament to the violence that had extinguished her young life. Blood mingled with the dark earth, a chilling reminder of the horror that had unfolded just hours before. The sight was horrific, leaving young Bobby paralyzed with shock, unable to process the enormity of what he had just discovered.

Investigators soon arrived, their solemn expressions reflecting the gravity of the situation. As they began to sift through the details of the scene, it became clear that this was no random act of violence. The brutality of the crime sent seismic waves of fear through the small town, where such horrors were almost unheard of. Mamie, who had been known for her kind spirit and infectious laughter, was a beloved figure in the community. The thought of her life being so violently cut short was unfathomable.

As the investigators meticulously examined the area, they painted a macabre picture that hinted at something more sinister than mere robbery. Mamie's diamond engagement ring sparkled on her finger, a symbol of love and commitment now tainted by blood. Next to it, her silver wedding band gleamed under the waning light, a cruel reminder of the future that had been so brutally stolen away. The juxtaposition of these precious items against the backdrop of her tragic demise was almost poetic in its horror, leaving the officers grappling for answers.

Nearby, her purse lay untouched, as if it had been placed there deliberately to send a message. Inside, a modest $9 in change jangled softly, accompanied by a pack of cigarettes and a wristwatch. The contents painted a vivid portrait of a life that, while ordinary, had been filled with aspirations and dreams. The scene was eerily quiet, broken only by the occasional rustle of leaves in the gentle evening breeze—an unsettling contrast to the violence that had occurred just moments before.

The town of Logan County, usually a peaceful place where neighbors greeted each other with warm smiles, was now engulfed in a thick fog of fear and uncertainty. Whispers filled the air, as residents speculated about the identity of Mamie's killer. The collective psyche of the town was shaken; they had lost more than just a cherished member of their community; they had lost their sense of safety and security.

As the investigation unfolded, the chilling details of Mamie's death clung to the town like a dark cloud. Her friends and family struggled to comprehend how someone so full of life could meet such a horrifying end. The images of her lifeless body, coupled with the gruesome details of her murder, would remain etched in their minds, serving as a constant reminder of the fragility of life and the lurking shadows of violence that could invade even the most serene settings. In a town where innocence had once reigned, the echoes of that fateful night would linger long after the sun set on June 21, 1932, a day that marked the end of Mamie Johnson's life and the beginning of a community's haunting nightmare.

The investigation quickly turned into a tangled web of intrigue and suspicion. Charles Stephenson, a handyman who had worked for Harry Robertson, was arrested and eventually convicted of Mamie's murder. But questions loomed large over the trial. The courtroom became a stage for a dramatic spectacle that drew standing-room-only crowds, eager to witness the unraveling of this tragic tale. Spectators brought their own chairs and picnic lunches, turning the trial into a community event. The air was thick with speculation and gossip, as whispers of Mamie's affairs and the involvement of powerful men echoed through the gallery.

As the trial unfolded, the brutality of Mamie's murder was juxtaposed with the mundane reality of courtroom proceedings. Onlookers were captivated by the details of the case, which revealed a chilling reality of betrayal and ambition. Morticians unearthed bloody rags and a razor from Harry Robertson's home, raising eyebrows and fuelling speculation that the investigation was more complicated than it appeared. The prosecutor painted a vivid picture of violence and betrayal, while the defense argued that Stephenson was merely a scapegoat for a crime committed by someone more powerful—someone who could manipulate the law and evade justice.

Despite Stephenson's conviction, the whispers didn't die down; they only grew louder. Was he truly guilty? Or had he been caught in a deadly game, a pawn manipulated by shadows lurking in the corners of Logan County? The ultimate fate of Mamie's remains further complicated the narrative. Her death certificate indicated she was buried at Logan Memorial Park, yet other records suggested her body was transported back to her roots in Bradfordsville, Kentucky. The mystery of her final resting place only served to stoke the fires of local legend.

Now, let's venture into the supernatural. If you ever find yourself driving along 22 Mine Road, prepare for a peculiar phenomenon that has captivated locals and ghost hunters alike. Legend has it that if you place your car in neutral on a hill near where Mamie's body was found, it will mysteriously roll uphill. Yes, uphill! Is it a clever trick of physics or is it the ghostly hand of Mamie giving you a gentle nudge, perhaps even a playful wink?

Drivers have reported strange occurrences, claiming to feel an inexplicable tug at their vehicles as they traverse the haunted roads. Coal truck drivers share eerie tales of picking up a woman in vintage attire, only to have her vanish from the cab moments later, leaving them bewildered and questioning their own sanity. Witnesses describe her spectral figure walking along the highway, dressed in the fashion of the early 1930s, her white dress fluttering in the night breeze, evoking a sense of both beauty and tragedy.

But the ghostly encounters don't stop there. Locals have shared spine-tingling stories of experiencing a sudden chill in the air, a tingling sensation running down their spines when passing by the area where Mamie was found. Some have reported seeing a faint light flickering in the distance, reminiscent of a lantern, guiding them through the darkness. Others describe a feeling of being watched, as if Mamie's spirit is observing from the shadows, forever searching for justice.

The legend of Mamie Thurman has transcended the realm of mere storytelling and has woven itself into the cultural fabric of Logan County. Inspired by her tale, local playwrights have penned plays, authors have crafted ghost stories, and thrill-seekers have flocked to the area, eager to catch a glimpse of the ghostly figure that has become a haunting symbol of unsolved mysteries. Her story continues to echo through the ages, reminding us of the fragility of life and the unrelenting quest for justice that transcends even death.

As we reach the end of our spooky journey down 22 Mine Road, one must ponder: what do we truly think about ghosts? Are they mere figments of our imagination, or do they serve as reminders of the tragedies that once unfolded in the very spots we tread? With Mamie Thurman's story echoing through the ages, it's hard not to wonder if her spirit still lingers, playfully toying with parked cars and ensuring her tale is never forgotten. So, dear readers, the next time you find yourself cruising down this haunted stretch of road, keep an eye on your rearview mirror—who knows what might be lurking just out of sight, ensuring Mamie's legacy continues to haunt us all?

THE PEOPLE IN WHITE

CHAPTER 3

THE PEOPLE IN WHITE

A real ghostly encounter

My grandfather has been gone for a number of years now, but the echo of his presence still resonates within me. He was more than just a grandfather; he was my father figure, my mentor, the kind of man whose wisdom I sought for almost every dilemma life threw my way. His loss, despite the stoic mask I wore in public, has profoundly affected me. I still find myself reaching for my phone, my thumb hovering over his name, longing to hear his voice and ask for his advice on the challenges I face. But alas, that's impossible now—except through prayer, of course.

In the last few years of his life, I witnessed a painful transformation. His faith, once a sturdy oak, began to wither as his body betrayed him. "It's hard to believe when your body screams otherwise," he once said, a shadow of sadness crossing his face as he struggled to find comfort in the chaos of pain. Before that decline, he was a man consumed by a deep curiosity about the universe and the divine. He studied various religions with a fervor that often left me in awe, claiming that understanding different perspectives brought him closer to his higher power.

I think much of this spiritual quest stemmed from an experience that haunted him long before I was even born. He'd been driving along one of Idaho's mountainous roads when something extraordinary happened. "You wouldn't believe it if I told you," he would start, his eyes twinkling with both wonder and a hint of dread. I remember leaning in, captivated, as he recounted how he lost control of the car, skidding perilously close to the edge of a steep drop. "I thought I was done for, but then," he paused, as if the memory still gripped him, "I felt this warmth, like a hand guiding me back."

Each time he told the story, I could see the same eerie chill wash over him, as if reliving that moment brought back the fear and the profound sense of something greater that he had felt. He believed it was a sign, a brush with the divine that ignited his lifelong quest for answers. "Maybe," he would say, "there's more to this life than we can see." That thought lingered in my mind long after he passed, a reminder that faith, like love, can endure even when the body fails.

The winding roads stretched ominously ahead of him, twisting like a restless serpent, and he clung to the hope that just around the next bend, the city of Boise would finally emerge, a beacon of certainty amidst this labyrinth of uncertainty. Yet, as he rounded yet another curve, he was met with the same relentless expanse of mountains, their rugged peaks silhouetted against the late afternoon sky. Each new view seemed to mock him—a reminder that he was still lost, still circling this vast wilderness.

How do you get lost on a road where the only options were to go one way or another?

He couldn't help but chuckle bitterly at the thought. It was a valid question, one he had asked himself repeatedly in the last hour. Yet here he was, utterly disoriented, with no signs of civilization in sight. The landscape was a relentless parade of trees and rocks, their untouched beauty underscored by his growing anxiety. He glanced down at the gas gauge, the needle sinking dangerously below half a tank. Panic simmered in his chest; if he had to turn back now, there was no way he would reach the previous town before the precious liquid ran dry, leaving him stranded in an unforgiving stretch of wilderness.

I could pull over and hope someone drives by to ask for directions…

Yet that thought felt more like a cruel joke than a viable plan. He hadn't seen another vehicle for almost an hour, and the solitary car that had passed him had been speeding in the opposite direction, a fleeting moment of hope that vanished as quickly as it had appeared. The road ahead seemed to stretch endlessly, a solitary ribbon of asphalt leading him further into the unknown. Perhaps there was a town somewhere ahead, or maybe it was just another dirt path veering off into the trees, leading to some hidden cabin where a hermit lived, blissfully unaware of his plight.

With no good options available, he settled on what he considered the least disastrous choice: to drive on until he either ran out of gas or stumbled upon the next town. The sun, now a fiery orb sinking toward the horizon, cast a warm glow over the mountains, but the beauty was lost on him. Shadows began to creep across the road like dark fingers, and with the encroaching dusk, a sense of foreboding settled over him. The air felt thicker, and the trees that lined the road seemed to lean in, as if whispering secrets he wasn't meant to hear.

A chill washed over him, and he glanced nervously at the rearview mirror, half-expecting to see headlights approaching, but the only thing staring back at him was his own weary reflection, eyes wide and haunted.

"Come on, just a little further," he muttered, the words feeling like a desperate prayer. The tension in the car was palpable, every creak of the vehicle amplifying his unease. He tightened his grip on the steering wheel, the faux leather cold beneath his palms. The fading light painted the world in shades of gray, and the isolation felt suffocating, as if the very mountains were closing in around him.

As the light diminished, he could have sworn he saw something dart between the trees—just a flicker, but it sent a shiver down his spine. He shook his head, dismissing it as a trick of the fading light, but doubt gnawed at him. The road ahead stretched into the darkening unknown, each passing moment eroding his resolve. What lay ahead? Was it salvation or something far more sinister? He had to believe that Boise was just around the corner, waiting to pull him from this suffocating uncertainty. But with each passing second, the mountains loomed larger, and his hope dimmed like the sun disappearing behind their jagged peaks.

The road began to rise gently, a gradual incline that seemed to stretch on forever beneath the vast, cerulean sky. As he crested the hill, an unusual sight emerged before him, stark against the muted greens and browns of the sagebrush and grasslands. A group of people, perhaps a dozen in number, moved gracefully through the vegetation, their bodies swathed in flowing white gowns that fluttered slightly in the warm breeze. There were men and women among them, and they moved with an ethereal quality that made the scene feel almost dreamlike.

At once, their heads turned in perfect synchrony, as if some unseen conductor had commanded their attention. His heart raced, and he felt goosebumps prickle along his arms, prickling like tiny electric shocks. The sensation was unsettling, as if they had turned to peer deep into his very soul.

Slowing down, he brought the car to a halt, the engine idling softly, the sound of it blending with the whisper of the wind. The group stepped closer to the edge of the road, their gazes locking onto him with an intensity that felt almost otherworldly. He shivered, his skin crawling under the weight of their unblinking stares. It was as if each pair of eyes was a mirror reflecting his innermost thoughts, his deepest fears.

Taking a deep breath, he rolled down the window, the mechanical whirring slicing through the silence. "Excuse me!" he called out, trying to sound casual despite the knot tightening in his stomach. His gaze fell upon a woman with long, flowing blonde hair that shimmered like spun gold in the sunlight. She stood slightly apart from the others, her warm smile contrasting sharply with the eerie atmosphere. "Can you tell me where I am?"

But she simply continued to stare, her expression unwavering, as if his words had not even registered. The others remained silent, their eyes still fixed on him, unyielding and inscrutable. Minutes ticked by, stretching into an uncomfortable silence, and he felt the weight of their gaze pressing down on him.

Frustrated and unnerved, he finally rolled up the

window, the glass sealing him off from the unsettling scene outside. He shifted the gear into drive, the car rolling forward, but his mind was racing. Where had they come from? He hadn't seen a car or house in the vicinity, and the isolation of the road only deepened the mystery.

A thought struck him suddenly—what if they needed help? The nagging feeling of responsibility tugged at him, and he couldn't shake the concern that he might be abandoning them, lost and alone in the vast expanse of the wilderness. With a decisive flick of the steering wheel, he turned the car around, the gravel crunching beneath the tires as he retraced his path back to the gathering. After all, they were on foot; it would be impossible for them to have traveled far.

As he drove back, he glanced out the windshield stiffened by anxiety, half-expecting to see them still standing there, their ethereal forms a haunting image against the vast backdrop of the landscape. What could compel a group to wander without the aid of modern transportation? The questions swirled in his mind like autumn leaves caught in a gusty wind, each one more perplexing than the last.

As he rounded the corner that led to the spot where

he had previously stopped, an unsettling sensation washed over him. The area lay completely deserted, an eerie stillness hanging in the air. He glanced around, taking in the wide-open views that stretched for nearly a mile on either side of the road. The vibrant hues of the autumn leaves fluttered in the gentle breeze, but there was no sign of life—no flicker of movement, no hint of the group he had witnessed moments earlier.

"Where could they have gone?" he muttered to himself, his voice barely breaking the silence. The bizarre sight of them, all clad in mismatched clothes, had been so vivid in his mind. They should have stood out starkly against the backdrop of nature, yet now they seemed to have vanished into thin air.

Driven by a mix of curiosity and a creeping sense of unease, he pressed the accelerator and drove a little further down the road, straining to catch a glimpse of anyone, anything. But again, there was nothing—just the whisper of the wind through the trees and the soft crunch of gravel beneath his tires.

"Great, just great," he sighed, feeling a twinge of irritation at having wasted precious time and fuel. He made a quick U-turn, the tires skidding slightly on the gravel, and headed back down the road. As he drove, a flicker of reassurance settled within him, a quiet voice whispering that perhaps everything would turn out just fine.

Fifteen minutes passed, the rhythmic hum of the engine lulling him into a state of calm. Each turn he took felt familiar, as if he were retracing the steps of an old memory. "Just keep going," he told himself, a mantra against the strange event.

Finally, after what felt like a thousand twists and turns, the first glimmers of city lights pierced the darkness ahead. They twinkled like stars fallen to Earth, a promise of home and safety. Relief washed over him as he realized he was almost there, the warmth of familiarity enveloping him like a well-worn blanket.

Later in life, my grandfather would often reflect on the strange event that unfolded that day, a memory etched into the fabric of his mind. As he sat on the worn, leather couch, his gaze drifting out the window, he would sometimes wonder aloud to anyone who cared to listen. "Do you think they were spirits or angels?" he would muse, a hint of awe in his voice. "Maybe they were just trying to tell me I was going to be okay."

He could still picture the figures, ethereal and shimmering, hovering at the edge of his vision. Their presence brought an unexpected calm, a stark contrast to the turmoil churning inside him. Despite the daunting circumstances he faced, he felt a warm embrace of tranquility wash over him.

One thing he was certain of was this: after he left that place, the feeling of peace that enveloped him was undeniable, even more so than the fear that should have gripped him. As he walked home, each step felt lighter, the weight of his worries lifting with every footfall. "You're not alone," he whispered to himself, recalling the fleeting faces that had offered him solace in a moment of despair.

What happened to my grandfather that day? I'm not entirely sure, but it was clear something extraordinary was looking out for him, guiding him home. Whether it was an angel or a spirit, the experience left an indelible mark on his heart. In the quiet moments of his later years, he would often whisper a simple thank you into the stillness, grateful for the unseen guardians that had watched over him.

PHANTOMS OF SUSCON

CHAPTER 4

PHANTOMS OF SUSCON

In the shadowy depths of Pittston Township, Pennsylvania, Suscon Road winds its way through gnarled trees and thick underbrush, a serpentine path that seems to beckon the unwary into its dark embrace. This long, twisting state route, which morphs into Thornhurst and Bear Lake Roads, pulses with an unsettling energy, as if the very ground beneath holds the weight of countless whispers and untold secrets. Eerie tales and ghostly encounters linger in the air, clinging to the fog like a shroud, making this haunted thoroughfare a chilling cornerstone of local legend and folklore.

The Black Bridge

At the heart of Suscon Road's haunted reputation lies the infamous Black Bridge, a once-sturdy railroad crossing that now stands as a mere ghost of its former self, long abandoned since its tragic demise in the 1980s. The bridge, now cloaked in a shroud of darkness and neglect, is a skeletal remnant of history; its wooden planks warped and splintered, groaning under the weight of time. Weeds snake through the cracks, and rusting iron beams jut out like jagged teeth, ready to devour the unwary. As night descends, the air thickens with an unsettling chill, and the low fog swirls around the bridge like a restless spirit, whispering secrets of the past.

Visitors frequently report bloodcurdling screams piercing the stillness of the night, reverberating through the dense trees that loom like sentinels over the road. These cries, chilling and raw, intertwine with the paralyzing tales of a spectral figure—a young woman clad in a flowing white dress, her wraithlike form gliding silently through the woods that cradle her tragedy. The fabric of her gown billows like mist, shimmering in the moonlight, leaving behind an ethereal glow that casts an eerie luminescence in the shadows.

The stories surrounding her are as varied as the leaves on the trees that envelop Suscon Road. Some say she is a jilted bride, her dreams of love transformed into a haunting sorrow, who chose the bridge as her final resting place. Her anguished spirit, forever entwined with the scent of wilting roses, roams the woods, clutching a wilted bouquet in her spectral hands. Others recount the sorrowful tale of a young girl tragically killed on prom night, her laughter silenced forever, still wandering the darkened path in search of a ride home, her soft sobs mingling with the rustling leaves.

Another legend speaks of a mother and child lost in a car crash, their spirits still tethered to the road, forever caught in an eternal embrace of grief. The air grows heavy with the scent of burnt rubber and despair, as their phantom forms flicker in and out of existence, looking for solace in an unforgiving world. Yet another tale whispers of a ghostly escapee from a nearby asylum, whose anguished cries echo through the night, a chilling reminder of her desperate leap from the bridge into the abyss below.

Regardless of which version captures the imagination, the haunting presence of the Suscon Screamer has sent shivers down the spines of many a local spook seeker, each recounting their spine-tingling encounters with a mix of fear and exhilaration. As the moon hangs low in the ink-black sky, casting an otherworldly glow, tales of the Black Bridge ripple through the air, weaving a tapestry of horror and wonder that lingers long after the last visitor departs. The very ground seems to pulse with the heartbeat of the past, echoing with whispered warnings, urging the brave and the foolish alike to tread cautiously in the realm of the restless dead.

The Eerie Soundscapes of Suscon Road

As the sun sinks beneath the horizon, casting long shadows that stretch like skeletal fingers across the cracked asphalt, the atmosphere thickens with a palpable tension. A peculiar ritual unfolds among the weary travelers: compelled by an unseen force, drivers instinctively lean on their horns, releasing three sharp blasts that pierce the heavy twilight air near the decrepit remains of the old Black Bridge. The bridge, draped in a cloak of creeping vines and rust, looms like a ghostly sentinel over the murky waters below, its once-proud structure now a relic of forgotten tales. Those who dare to partake in this local custom may find themselves haunted by the chilling screams of the Suscon Screamer, a sound that ripples through the trees like an ominous wave crashing against the shore of sanity.

The cries pierce the stillness, slicing through the encroaching darkness with an unsettling clarity. They echo off the gnarled trunks of ancient trees, warped and twisted as if in pain, their branches clawing at the sky in a desperate bid for escape. Each scream seems to resonate from a deep, unfathomable abyss, wrapping around the listener like a shroud, instilling a sense of dread that lingers long after the sound has faded. As night falls, the air becomes thick with an unsettling energy, electrified by the unseen and the unknown, where shadows dance just beyond the reach of the headlights, teasing the imaginations of those brave enough to venture forth.

But it is not merely the spectral cries that send shivers down the spine; the whispers of something more sinister linger in the air. Some locals suggest that the source of these eerie sounds might not be human at all. Rumors swirl like fog around a strange creature—a grotesque amalgamation of man and beast, a half-human, half-pig swamp monster, said to dwell in the fetid marshlands nearby. Its guttural growls are woven into the night, a dark symphony that melds with the rustling leaves, hinting at something far more primal lurking in the shadows.

Others speculate about the legend of a long-lost lion, an exotic beast that escaped from a traveling circus decades ago. Its roars, once majestic, have morphed into haunting screams, echoing through the night like a mournful dirge. This blend of myths adds an extra layer of intrigue, ensuring that Suscon Road remains a focal point of supernatural speculation.

As the night deepens, the road twists and turns like a serpent, guiding the unsuspecting towards its sinister heart. The flickering streetlights cast eerie shadows that stretch and contort, creating fleeting figures that vanish as quickly as they appear. Each bend in the road feels like an invitation to the abyss, where reality blurs and the line between the seen and unseen dissolves into the encroaching darkness. Here, on Suscon Road, the air is thick with stories untold, waiting for the next traveler to awaken the echoes of the past—remnants of a world where fear reigns and the night is alive with the whispers of the damned.

The Suscon Sasquatch and Other Oddities

The whispers of the Suscon Screamer are merely the prelude to a symphony of the strange that haunts the shadowy woods and murky banks of Suscon Lake. Here, in the twilight hours when the sun surrenders to the creeping darkness, the air thickens with an unsettling energy, and the rustling leaves seem to whisper secrets of eldritch beings that defy the natural order.

In May of 1976, a family seeking solace by the lake stumbled upon an encounter that would forever etch itself into their memories. As they picnicked beneath the gnarled branches of ancient trees, their laughter was abruptly silenced by an unsettling rustle in the underbrush. Emerging from the tangled thicket, a family of four impossibly large, hairy beings stepped into view. Towering at least six feet tall, their bodies were cloaked in matted, dark fur that glistened with the sheen of damp earth, reflecting the fading light like shadowy specters. The creatures moved with a deliberate grace, their long limbs bending beneath the weight of a world that felt foreign and ancient. Their eyes—deep and haunting, like pools of obsidian—seemed to drink in the family's astonishment, a moment suspended in time where the line between the natural and the supernatural blurred into an unsettling haze. The air grew thick with an unnameable tension, and the family, frozen in a tableau of awe and terror, watched as the beings slowly melted back into the shadows, leaving behind only the echoes of their existence—a rustle of leaves, a tremor in the earth.

But the eerie tales do not end there. The woods surrounding Suscon Lake are also home to whispered accounts of a monstrous creature that prowls the dense forest, lurking just beyond the reach of the light. A local hunter, with eyes that had seen the depths of many a dark night, recounted a harrowing encounter with this aberrant entity. He described a creature that sprawled in the undergrowth, stretching a terrifying six feet long, its elongated form twisted and grotesque. Its snout, elongated and glistening with moisture, sniffed the air like a predator assessing its prey. The gray fur that cloaked its body rippled like the surface of a disturbed pond, and its feet—webbed and clawed—left deep, unsettling prints in the soft earth, as if the very ground recoiled from its touch.

The hunter's voice trembled as he spoke, painting vivid images of the creature's haunting presence, its eyes glinting like shards of ice under the moonlight, filled with an intelligence that sent chills down his spine. The community buzzed with unease, the hunter's tale igniting a primal fear of the unknown that lurked in the shadows of Suscon Road. What otherworldly beings roamed these darkened woods, and what dark secrets did they guard? As night fell and the fog rolled in, the whispers of the Suscon

Sasquatch and its sinister companions intertwined, beckoning the brave and the foolish alike into a realm where reality blurred into nightmare, and the echoes of the unknown reverberated through the stillness of the night.

The Streetlights of Mystery

The streetlights lining Suscon Road stand like sentinels, their flickering bulbs casting a ghostly pallor over the cracked pavement. Locals whisper of the eighteen iron poles that frame the road, each one a twisted silhouette against the deepening twilight. Yet, in a bizarre twist of fate, eleven of these lights remain stubbornly extinguished, their darkened globes resembling vacant eyes watching the world with a malevolent curiosity.

Every night, the same eleven lights succumb to an unholy darkness, their feeble flickers snuffed out as if by an unseen hand. The remaining seven cast an uneven glow, illuminating patches of the asphalt while leaving yawning chasms of shadow that seem to pulse with an unsettling life of their own. As pedestrians pass, they can't shake the feeling that something lurks just beyond the reach of the light, waiting and watching.

With each passing day, the cycle continues—different lights flicker to life, only to be consumed by night's embrace once more. The locals, caught between bemusement and dread, ponder if this dance of light and shadow is merely a trick of fate or a sinister omen, beckoning them deeper into the enigma that is Suscon Road. Whispers of ghostly figures and inexplicable sounds swirl through the community, intertwining with the very fabric of their reality, as the streetlights stand witness to secrets that may never be unveiled.

The Smurl Haunting

Nestled just beyond the whispers of Suscon Road, where shadows mingle with the remnants of the past, lies a tale that chills the very marrow of the bones—the Smurl Haunting. In 1986, the Smurl family of West Pittston unwittingly invited the macabre into their lives when they settled into their unassuming double-block home, a place that soon transformed from a sanctuary into a theater of terror.

The air within those walls grew heavy, thick with an unshakable sense of dread. At first, it was the unsettling creaks and groans of the house settling—sounds that echoed like the soft cries of lost souls. But as night fell and darkness draped over the neighborhood, the disturbances escalated into a cacophony of chaos. The family soon found themselves tormented by abrupt, bone-rattling noises, like the angry clattering of furniture, and whispers that slithered through the air, chilling them to the core. Most horrifying of all, a family member was hurled down the steep, unyielding staircase, as if an invisible hand had seized them and flung them into the abyss. It was a harrowing spectacle that turned their lives into a waking nightmare.

Desperate for salvation, the Smurls reached out to renowned demonologists Ed and Lorraine Warren, whose very presence seemed to summon an uneasy tension. The Warrens, armed with their sage and solemnity, investigated the house and bore witness to the supernatural chaos. They confirmed that the Smurls were not alone; three spirits wandered the halls, but one was particularly sinister—a malevolent force that thrived on their fear, feeding off their despair like a dark parasite.

With a series of exorcisms that echoed with fervent prayers and the crackling of holy water, the family clung to hope, but each attempt only yielded brief respite. The entity, a shadowy figure cloaked in malice, returned with a vengeance, unleashing further torment and despair. Their home, once a refuge, became a magnet for thrill-seekers and ghost hunters, drawn by the magnetic pull of the supernatural, eager to witness the horrors that had unfolded within those walls.

Even a third exorcism, steeped in desperation and the fervor of faith, seemed only to offer a temporary balm. The horrors resurfaced with a relentless ferocity, prompting the Smurls to abandon their haunted abode in search of solace and safety, fleeing into the unknown. Their harrowing saga culminated in the publication of "The Haunted," a chilling account that wove their miseries into the fabric of local folklore, ensuring that their tale would echo through the ages.

In 1991, the haunting was immortalized on the silver screen, a grim adaptation that brought their terrifying experiences to life, further entrenching the Smurl haunting as a cornerstone of NEPA ghost lore. Today, the very name conjures images of shadowy figures lurking in corners, flickering lights, and the anguished cries of a family forever marked by their brush with the supernatural. The Smurl Haunting remains a grim reminder that some stories should never be told, lest the darkness they harbor be awakened once more.

The Intersection of Tragedy and the Supernatural

The stories of Suscon Road and the Smurl haunting intertwine in an intricate tapestry of tragedy, loss, and the inexplicable. Each tale reflects the human spirit's desire to understand the unknown, to find meaning in the chaos of existence. As the Suscon Screamer wanders the woods in her flowing white dress, searching for closure, the Smurl family's ordeal highlights the darker aspects of the supernatural, where malevolent forces lurk behind closed doors.

The allure of Suscon Road lies not only in its ghostly tales but also in the exploration of fear itself. What is it about the unknown that draws people in, even as it sends shivers down their spines? Perhaps it is the thrill of the chase, the exhilaration of standing on the precipice between reality and the supernatural, where every rustle in the bushes could be a ghost or a long-lost creature waiting to share its story.

An Invitation to the Curious

For those brave enough to test the waters of Suscon Road, the journey promises an adventure steeped in mystery and allure. As dusk falls and the air thickens with anticipation, the road beckons, inviting curious souls to partake in its eerie rituals. Whether it's the chilling screams of the Suscon Screamer, the fleeting shadows of mysterious creatures, or the flickering streetlights that dance in and out of existence, each visit becomes a chapter in an ongoing story of the inexplicable.

As the line between reality and myth blurs on Suscon Road, thrill-seekers and ghost hunters alike find themselves caught in an intoxicating spiral of fear and fascination. It's a place where the past lingers, where the whispers of lost souls echo, and where every adventure unfolds with a delicious blend of spookiness and delight.

So, for those who dare to venture forth, remember to keep your eyes peeled and your senses alert. You never know what might be lurking just beyond the trees, waiting to share its tale—or perhaps, to add your own story to the eerie legacy of Suscon Road.

THE GHOSTLY HITCHHIKER

CHAPTER 5

THE GHOSTLY HITCHHIKER

In the heart of Guilford County, North Carolina, lies a stretch of asphalt that has earned a reputation steeped in mystery and spectral tales. Jamestown Road—the very name sends a shiver down the spine of the uninitiated, inviting them into a world where the veil between the living and the dead is tantalizingly thin. With its lush canopies, winding paths, and the remnants of an old bridge, this road embodies an eerie charm. Yet, it is the haunting legend of a ghostly hitchhiker known as "Lydia" that keeps the locals both wary and intrigued.

The Enigmatic Lydia

As dusk descends, the atmosphere along Jamestown Road morphs from the mundane into something otherworldly, enveloped in an ethereal haze that seems to echo with the whispers of the past. The air grows thick with anticipation, as if the very ground holds its breath, waiting for the spectral events of the night. It is during these fog-laden evenings, when the world is draped in a silvery shroud, that Lydia, the ghostly figure in a flowing blue dress, is said to make her haunting appearance.

Emerging from the mist, she stands beside the road, her ethereal form flickering like a candle in a draft, illuminated momentarily by the fleeting glow of passing headlights. Her dress, tattered and translucent, flows around her like vapor, intertwining with the fog as if she is part of it. The soft, ghostly light reveals her pallid skin, a stark contrast against the darkening surroundings, and her long hair, once vibrant, now cascades like wisps of smoke down her back. Residents who have encountered her recount tales of her desperate attempts to flag down motorists, her eyes wide with a blend of sorrow and longing, glistening like dew on a cold morning.

The origins of Lydia's tragic tale trace back to the roaring 1920s, a decade filled with hope and heartbreak. According to local lore, she was a vivacious young woman, brimming with dreams, who perished in a car accident while en route to a grand dance—perhaps the prom of her youth. That fateful night, rain-soaked roads glistened under the pale moonlight, transforming into treacherous ribbons of reflection. Youthful exuberance collided with the harsh reality of fate, resulting in a catastrophic wreck that claimed her life, leaving behind echoes of laughter and music that would never again fill the night air.

Now, her spirit wanders the very path she once traveled, trapped in a liminal space, endlessly searching for a way home. The scent of damp earth and decaying leaves mingles with the chill in the air, creating a suffocating atmosphere that hangs heavy around her. As she raises her delicate hand to signal passing cars, a chilling breeze carries the faint strains of a long-forgotten melody, hinting at the dance she never reached.

Those who have dared to stop for her often report feeling an overwhelming sense of despair wash over them, as if they, too, are compelled to share in her grief. Shadows seem to stretch unnaturally, and the night grows eerily silent, as if the world itself momentarily pauses to witness her plight. With each passing vehicle, her form flickers and fades, leaving behind a lingering sense of unease—a reminder that sometimes, the past refuses to let go, and lost souls remain bound to the roads they once traveled. As dawn begins to break, the fog dissipates, but the haunting image of Lydia remains etched in the minds of those who encounter her, a spectral guardian of memories that refuse to fade.

The First Sighting: A Chilling Encounter

The first documented sighting of Lydia took place in 1924, as chronicled by North Carolina folklorist Nancy Roberts in her 1959 work, An Illustrated Guide to Ghosts & Mysterious Occurrences in the Old North State. A student named Burke Hardison was driving home to High Point that night when he spotted a girl in a white gown, drenched by the rain and seemingly lost. He stopped to offer assistance, only to find that once he reached his destination, she had vanished into thin air.

When he knocked on the door of a nearby house, seeking answers, he was met with chilling news: the girl he had aided had died in a tragic accident the previous year. The realization sent a wave of unease rippling through him, and thus the legend of Lydia began to take root in the collective consciousness of the area.

The Allure of the Vanishing Hitchhiker

Lydia's story is part of a broader tapestry woven with folklore and urban legends, echoing the age-old tale of the "Vanishing Hitchhiker." Folklorists Rosalie Hankey and Richard Beasley cataloged similar narratives in their 1943 study, exploring the uncanny intersections of life, death, and the unknown. These tales resonate with humanity's intrinsic curiosity about the afterlife and our fear of the unknown. Lydia's plight embodies this duality; she is both a tragic figure and a harbinger of the eerie.

The Ghostly Bridge: A Haunting Location

The haunting backdrop of Lydia's tale is none other than the old bridge that stands as a silent witness to the passage of time. Cloaked in vines and overgrowth, the abandoned structure looms ominously over the landscape. The bridge, once bustling with vehicles, now exists as a graffiti shrine—a canvas for local artists who pay homage to the legend of Lydia. Each spray-painted tribute adds to the lore, an ever-evolving testament to the ghostly presence that lingers in the air.

Visitors often report a palpable shift in energy as they approach the underpass. A chill dances along the spine, and the rustling leaves seem to whisper secrets long buried. Some brave souls have ventured there at night, armed with nothing but flashlights and a sense of adventure, hoping to catch a glimpse of the forlorn figure. Those who claim to have seen her describe a deep sense of sadness emanating from Lydia, a reflection of her eternal quest for closure.

The Intersection of Tragedy and the Supernatural

While Lydia's haunting captivates the imagination, the road beneath her ghostly presence is steeped in a history far darker than mere whispers of the supernatural. Jamestown Road, flanked by gnarled trees that loom like skeletal sentinels, has borne witness to a tapestry of tragedies woven with threads of despair, accidents, and unspeakable crimes—each event casting a long shadow that contributes to its eerie reputation. The air thickens with foreboding, and as twilight descends, the road transforms into a realm where the living tread lightly, aware they are not alone. The chilling winds seem to carry echoes of the past, intertwining Lydia's tale with the mournful cries of souls lost too soon.

Local historians Amy Greer and Michael Renegar have plunged into the murky depths of time, unearthing fragments of the past that hint at the restless spirits within the shadows. Their investigations led them to a yellowed newspaper article from 1920, detailing the tragic death of a young woman named Annie Jackson. The ink stains tell a story of sorrow, revealing that she met her doom in a car accident just three miles from the haunted stretch of road, her life extinguished by a treacherous combination of rain-slicked pavement and sheer misfortune. The haunting image of her vehicle, a ghostly silhouette against the downpour, lingers in the mind. Could Annie, with her dreams washed away, be the true identity behind the enigma of Lydia? The fog of uncertainty cloaks the truth, deepening the mystery with every passing year.

The Psychological Pull of Fear and Curiosity

The tales surrounding Jamestown Road awaken a profound introspection about the nature of fear and curiosity. Why do we find ourselves irresistibly drawn to the macabre, to the mysteries that swirl like mist around the living and the dead? There's an undeniable thrill in the unknown, a magnetic pull that compels souls to seek out haunted locations where shadows breathe and whispers linger. Lydia's story serves not only as a ghostly reminder of life's fragility but also as a spectral mirror reflecting the haunting questions that stretch far beyond the grave.

As night envelops the road, small gatherings of thrill-seekers and curious minds emerge, their laughter mingling uneasily with shivers of fear. They share ghost stories, their voices rising and falling like the wind, acknowledging the absurdity of standing in the presence of a phantom while debating whether to laugh or scream. It becomes a classic case of human psychology, where fear entwines with fascination, creating a dance as old as time itself. The absurdity of seeking out a spectral hitchhiker evokes a poignant reflection of our quest for meaning in a world suffused with uncertainties. Each heartbeat resonates with the echo of Lydia's story, a chilling reminder that the line between life and death is as thin as the mist that clings to Jamestown Road—a road forever haunted by the burden of its past.

The Legacy of Jamestown Road

Today, Jamestown Road is not just a thoroughfare;

it has evolved into a cultural phenomenon, a hotspot for thrill-seekers and ghost hunters alike. Lydia's legend continues to be retold, each retelling adding a fresh layer to her story. Visitors come armed with cameras, hoping to capture the elusive spirit, while locals offer bemused smiles, their eyes glinting with a mix of skepticism and belief.

As night falls over Jamestown Road, the air stiffens with anticipation. The shadows dance under the glow of streetlights, and the sound of rustling leaves plays a haunting melody. The road may seem ordinary by day, but as darkness descends, it transforms into a portal to the past—a place where the living and the dead converge.

In the end, Jamestown Road remains a testament to the enduring power of storytelling. Whether one believes in Lydia's spirit or not, the allure of the road lies in its ability to spark the imagination, inviting all who traverse it to ponder the mysteries of life, death, and everything in between. After all, who among us can resist the thrill of a ghostly hitchhiker on a foggy night? As they say, curiosity killed the cat—but perhaps it also brings the spirit back to life.

CLINTON'S WHISPERS IN DARKNESS

CHAPTER 6

CLINTON'S WHISPERS IN DARKNESS

In the heart of West Milford, New Jersey, lies a ten-mile stretch of asphalt that casts a long shadow in the annals of American folklore: Clinton Road. At first glance, it appears to be just another winding country lane, flanked by dense forests and the occasional glimpse of a shimmering lake. However, as dusk descends, the landscape transforms. The trees grow tall and twisted, their gnarled branches reaching out like skeletal fingers, while the shadows lengthen and dance across the pavement. This is no ordinary road; it is an enigmatic corridor steeped in haunting tales, chilling legends, and a history that raises the hairs on the back of one's neck.

The Road Less Traveled

Clinton Road is not just a route; it is a journey into the unknown. With its long, desolate stretches and a notable lack of civilization, it invites the curious and the intrepid. Local law enforcement has aptly described it as a place where "the imagination goes nuts." As cars roll by, the inhabitants of the woods seem to watch, their eyes glinting in the darkness, creating an atmosphere thick with suspense. The road is lined with whispers of the past, each bend and curve carrying the weight of unsolved mysteries and ghostly apparitions.

Ghost Boy Bridge

Perhaps the most infamous legend associated with Clinton Road is that of the Ghost Boy, a spectral figure forever haunting the rickety bridge that looms over the treacherous waters beneath, near the ominously dubbed "Dead Man's Curve." The tale whispers of a tragic fate, where the boy either slipped into the icy, swirling depths below or leapt to escape the screeching tires of an oncoming vehicle. Now, his restless spirit lingers, a wisp of sorrow in the night, said to return any coin tossed into the murky water—a peculiar twist of fate that entwines the living with the lost.

As midnight approaches, a shroud of thick fog envelops the bridge, and brave souls gather, hearts pounding like a war drum. They clutch their coins, fingers trembling, as shadows dance around them. One by one, they cast their offerings into the dark abyss below, where the water churns like the memories of the boy's last moments. Eerie silence blankets the night, broken only by the soft splash of metal meeting liquid. Those who dare to linger claim to glimpse a fleeting figure rising from the depths, its form shrouded in mist, pale as the moon above. Others insist they've felt an inexplicable tug at their sleeves, a gentle push as if the boy, still protecting what he lost, urges them away from the precipice. The water, dark and foreboding, reflects not only the moonlight but also the unending sorrow of a soul trapped between worlds, yearning for peace yet bound to the bridge, forever entwined with the living who dare to remember him.

Ruins of Cross Castle

Just a stone's throw from the desolate expanse of Clinton Road lies the haunting remains of Cross

Castle, a once-majestic estate built in 1905 by the enigmatic Richard Cross. What was once a proud three-story structure, adorned with intricate stonework and towering spires, now stands as a crumbling specter of its former glory. Vines creep up the weathered walls, their sinewy tendrils encasing the stone in a suffocating embrace, as if nature herself seeks to reclaim what was never meant to be. The air is thick with the scent of damp earth and decay, an olfactory reminder of the castle's long-forgotten opulence.

The castle's storied past is darkened by fire and neglect, its grandeur overshadowed by the sinister whispers of those who once gathered in its shadowy halls. Rumors swirl like autumn leaves in the wind, claiming that the KKK and devil worshipers convened here under the cloak of night, their rituals drenched in blood and malevolence. Flickering candlelight would cast monstrous shadows on the walls, and the echo of chanting would rise like smoke, curling into the night sky, mingling with the cries of lost souls.

Those who dare to wander close enough to the ruins often report hearing haunting chants reverberate through the trees, a ghostly chorus echoing the madness of past ceremonies. It is as if the very stones of Cross Castle retain the echoes of despair, each sound a reminder of the darkness that once thrived within its walls. The laughter of unseen figures dances on the wind, a chilling symphony that sends shivers racing down the spine, as if the castle itself is alive with the memories of its tainted history.

In the forest that encircles the castle, the trees stand like silent sentinels, their gnarled branches casting twisted shadows on the ground. Some intrepid souls have stumbled upon strange symbols etched into the bark, cryptic markings that whisper tales of ancient rites and dark pacts forged in secrecy. The air crackles with an energy that feels both electric and suffocating, as if the very atmosphere is heavy with the weight of forgotten curses.

As twilight descends, a thick fog unfurls from the underbrush, swirling around the ruins like a ghostly shroud. The sun sinks low, casting long, distorted shadows that stretch across the ground, creating the illusion of figures lurking just beyond the reach of light. Eyes seem to watch from the darkness, and the rustle of leaves hints at movement where none should be. The castle stands as a grim reminder of what lingers in the unseen—a place where the past refuses to fade, and the echoes of despair resonate eternally within the stone walls, waiting for the next curious soul to awaken the horrors that lie dormant.

Enigmatic Furnace

Nestled beyond the somber silhouette of Cross Castle, shrouded in the creeping tendrils of fog, lies a relic of Clinton Road's haunted legacy: the Furnace, an 18th-century iron smelter. Locals, with furtive glances and hushed voices, refer to it as the "Druidic Temple," a name steeped in whispered legends of dark rituals conducted by ancient Druids who once roamed these forsaken woods. The heavy stone structure, now a mere shadow of its former glory, stands defiantly against the encroaching wilderness, its weathered façade draped in a thick cloak of moss and ivy that seem to writhe like fingers in the wind.

As one approaches, the air thickens, laden with an oppressive weight that hangs heavily like storm clouds pregnant with rain. The Furnace looms ominously, its gaping archways resembling the hungry maws of a beast waiting to swallow the unwary. Fenced off with rusted iron bars that bend and twist like the gnarled roots of ancient trees, the boundary serves as a futile barrier against the insatiable curiosity of those drawn to its sinister allure. Yet, for the brave— or perhaps the foolish—

who dare to inch closer, an unsettling energy pulsates from within, as if the very stones themselves are alive, breathing with a life of their own.

The locals tell tales of those who have ventured too close, their voices trembling with fear as they recount the misfortunes that befell them. A man who entered seeking adventure returned with a pallor that spoke of nightmares; a group of teenagers, once carefree, emerged with shadows under their eyes, as if they had glimpsed something unspeakable lurking just beyond the veil of reality. Stories of strange illnesses, debilitating migraines, and inexplicable accidents swirl through the community like an unending storm, each tale more chilling than the last.

As dusk descends, the Furnace appears to exude an ethereal glow, a ghostly luminescence that beckons the curious into its embrace. Those who linger too long claim to hear whispers—soft, sibilant voices that curl around their minds like smoke, urging them to enter, to discover the secrets hidden within the crumbling walls. But what darkness resides within? What ancient power lies dormant, waiting to awaken? The air grows thick with dread, a palpable reminder that some doors, once opened, are not easily closed. And as the last rays of sunlight fade, the Furnace stands sentinel, its secrets cloaked in shadow, eternally guarding the malevolence that festers within.

The Iceman's Dark Legacy

Clinton Road stretches like a shadowy serpent through the heart of the New Jersey woods, its winding path shrouded in an unsettling stillness that seems to swallow sound itself. The trees, gnarled and twisted, loom overhead like the skeletal fingers of a long-abandoned graveyard, their branches clawing at the sky. Here, whispers of the supernatural intertwine with the echoes of very real horrors, creating a tapestry of dread that hangs heavy in the humid air.

In May of 1983, the tranquility of this desolate stretch was shattered by a cyclist, a solitary figure lost in the rhythm of his pedals. As he navigated the serpentine road, a dark omen sliced through the serenity: a flock of vultures, ominously circling, their wings casting fleeting shadows upon the ground. Intrigued yet filled with an instinctual dread, he felt an irresistible pull towards the source of their macabre congregation. The underbrush rustled with a sinister energy, as if the forest itself were holding its breath.

What he found would haunt him for a lifetime—a garbage bag, grotesquely disfigured, with a human head protruding at an unnatural angle, staring vacantly into the abyss. The sight was a jarring contrast to the natural beauty surrounding it, a grotesque reminder that death can lurk within the most serene of settings. The cyclist's heart raced, pounding a frantic rhythm against the silence of the woods, as he stumbled back, overwhelmed by the reality of what he had uncovered.

The victim was soon identified as Daniel Deppner, a man whose life had been irrevocably entwined with the dark underbelly of organized crime. His connection to Richard Kuklinski, the infamous mob hitman known as the "Iceman," sent shockwaves through the community. Kuklinski, a figure cloaked in chilling legend, had earned his nickname not just for his cold demeanor but for his gruesome method of freezing his victims, a tactic designed to obscure the time of death and instill terror in those who dared to cross him.

As the police investigation unfurled like a grotesque flower, it revealed a chilling textile woven with threads of betrayal, violence, and a ruthless quest for power. The deeper they delved, the more the sinister legacy of Kuklinski emerged—his confessions revealing a sordid history of multiple murders that painted him as one of the most notorious hitmen in American history. Each revelation was a drop of ice water cascading down the spine of the community, awakening a primal fear that the darkness was not merely a haunting tale but a living nightmare.

Clinton Road, already steeped in eerie folklore, now bore the weight of this grim reality, each mile echoing with the whispers of those who had vanished into the shadows. The air grew thick with a sense of foreboding, as if the very ground beneath was stained with the blood of the fallen. The road became a chilling reminder that true horror often lurks beneath the surface, waiting patiently to be uncovered, lying in wait for the next unsuspecting traveler who dares to venture into its haunted embrace.

Shadows of the Past

The haunted aura of Clinton Road is amplified by the shadows of its past. The road has long been a gathering place for those drawn to the macabre—from thrill-seekers hoping to catch a glimpse of the paranormal to those investigating the darker aspects of human nature. The intersection of tragedy and the supernatural creates a rich narrative that resonates deeply with those willing to explore.

Reports of ghostly figures, unearthly creatures, and inexplicable phenomena abound, leaving many to wonder: what draws these spirits to this lonely stretch of road? Is it the weight of unresolved tragedies, the echo of rituals long forgotten, or perhaps the very earth itself that holds their memories captive?

Paranormal Tales

The infamous ghost boy isn't the only haunt on the road. Legend has it that two park rangers were killed just off the road, and that they still patrol the area, their spirits forever bound to the soil they once protected. Park rangers, known for their service and dedication, are said to linger, maintaining an ethereal watch over the woods. Visitors have reported seeing shadowy figures darting between the trees, accompanied by a sense of being observed—a chilling reminder that some guardians never truly leave.

Haunted Surroundings

While anyone can drive down this dark road, those

wishing to explore the surrounding area on foot must first secure a hiking permit, a small barrier to the curious eager to uncover the secrets nestled within the woods. The dense forest surrounding Clinton Road is home to the ruins of Clinton Ironworks, several abandoned homes, a reservoir, and small ponds that hold their own mysteries. Each twist and turn through the underbrush unveils remnants of the past— rusted machinery, crumbling walls, and nature reclaiming what was once man-made.

Brave explorers often recount their experiences navigating the trails, where the air is thick with the scent of damp earth and the distant rustle of leaves adds an eerie soundtrack to their adventure. Shadows flicker between the trees, igniting the imagination. Are those merely the playful movements of wildlife, or something far more sinister? Each step taken in this haunted woodland is accompanied by an ever-present sense of anticipation, where the thrill of discovery tangles with an underlying fear of what may lurk just out of sight.

The Jersey Devil and Other Cryptids

Amidst the chilling legends that cling like fog to the winding paths of Clinton Road, tales of cryptids and otherworldly beings emerge from the shadows, each more unsettling than the last. The air is thick with an unease that seems to whisper through the gnarled branches overhead, where the Jersey Devil, a creature steeped in local folklore, is said to dwell. This winged specter, half beast and half nightmare, haunts the dense thickets, its presence a haunting echo of fear and fascination that sends shivers racing down the spine of anyone brave enough to tread these haunted grounds.

Witnesses, their voices trembling like autumn leaves in a wicked breeze, describe the Jersey Devil as a grotesque figure—an unholy amalgamation of creature and myth. With leathery wings that stretch like shadows against the moonlit sky and eyes that gleam with an otherworldly hunger, it prowls the underbrush, an embodiment of nature's darkest secrets. The very trees seem to recoil at its approach, their twisted limbs reaching out as if to ward off the unspeakable horror that lurks just beyond the periphery of sight. Its cry, a chilling blend of wails and screeches, pierces the stillness of the night, echoing through the darkness like the cries of lost souls searching for salvation.

The tales of the Jersey Devil weave seamlessly into the fabric of ghostly narratives that permeate the landscape, creating a rich tapestry of lore that captivates the imagination and ensnares the heart. Each story is a thread, binding the past to the present, infusing the very essence of Clinton Road with a palpable sense of dread. The line between reality and myth blurs here, as spectral apparitions and cryptids dance together in a macabre waltz, inviting both curiosity and fear in equal measure.

As twilight descends, the road transforms into a realm of shadows, where every rustle of leaves and distant snap of a twig heightens the pulse of primal fear. The very essence of Clinton Road becomes a mirror, reflecting humanity's deep-seated fascination with the unknown—a haunting desire to confront our darkest fears while simultaneously courting the thrill of the inexplicable. In this eerie landscape, the Jersey Devil is not merely a creature of folklore; it is a living embodiment of our deepest nightmares, lurking just beyond the veil of reality, waiting for the unwary to stumble into its waiting embrace. Each flicker of movement, each chilling sound, pulls at the threads of sanity, urging us to explore the depths of our fears, even as we long to flee.

Fear and Curiosity

The allure of Clinton Road lies in its ability to evoke a sense of wonder and dread simultaneously. It is a place where the mundane meets the extraordinary, where the thrill of the unknown beckons. As visitors navigate the winding path, their hearts race with the anticipation of what might lie ahead: a glimpse of the ghost boy, the echo of laughter from Cross Castle, or perhaps the rustle of unseen creatures in the underbrush.

Yet, amidst the thrill, there is a quiet introspection. What is it about fear that draws people in? The desire to confront the unknown is a universal impulse— a tantalizing blend of bravery and foolishness. In our quest for understanding, we often find ourselves standing at the precipice, balancing on the edge of curiosity and trepidation, contemplating the shadows that flicker just beyond our vision.

Clinton Road, with its eerie legends and dark history, stands as a testament to the power of storytelling. It is a place where the whispers of the past resonate through the trees, where the boundaries between life and death blur, and where the human experience is forever intertwined with the supernatural.

As the sun sets and the road transforms into a corridor of shadows, the tales of ghostly encounters, tragic histories, and cryptic mysteries continue to captivate those who dare to venture forth. Whether one seeks a thrill, a glimpse into the unknown, or simply a story to tell, Clinton Road promises an adventure—a haunting exploration of what lies beyond the veil of the ordinary.

So, for those brave enough to traverse this legendary road, remember: the shadows may be watching, and the tales may be more than mere stories. In the heart of West Milford, the spirit of Clinton Road lives on, inviting all who seek to uncover its secrets— with a wink of the eye and a chill down the spine.

THE TRAVELER

CHAPTER 7

THE TRAVELER

A real ghostly encounter

A couple of months ago, my friend Alex and I were driving down a winding road that cut through the northern part of California, meandering across southeastern Oregon and into Idaho. The scenery was stunning, with tall pines lining the highway and distant mountains peeking through the haze. But this particular highway was primarily a lifeline for the logging industry and a parade of eighteen-wheelers hauling their hefty loads across the continental United States. As I drove, I could feel the weight of the road beneath us, a seemingly endless stretch that felt both isolating and expansive.

I still remembered the guy behind the counter at the gas station we had stopped at earlier. He had leaned against the counter, arms crossed, a serious look etched across his weathered face. "You boys heading out on that road?" he asked, raising an eyebrow. "It's a long stretch out there, with hardly a place to stop. If you get stranded at night, well, you might be waiting quite a while before someone comes by."

I shrugged, trying to brush off his words. "We'll be fine. I've got a fairly new vehicle and almost a full tank of gas," I assured him, glancing at Alex, who was busy scrolling through his phone. "Right, Alex?"

"Yeah, man, no worries!" he replied, looking up with a grin. "Besides, we've got cell service. What could go wrong?"

Despite my bravado, as the hours rolled on, I began to feel the weight of his warning settle in my gut. The sun dipped lower in the sky, casting long shadows across the asphalt, and I was starting to realize just how true the clerk's words had been. I glanced around, my heart sinking a little. I'd only seen a couple of cars heading in the opposite direction, and the desolation was palpable. In fact, I hadn't seen any headlights behind us or in front of us for what felt like an eternity. The silence outside was almost deafening, broken only by the rhythmic hum of our tires against the road.

"Hey, do you think we should turn back?" I asked, half-joking, but Alex just laughed, shaking his head.

"Come on, we can't let a little isolation scare us off! This is an adventure!" he exclaimed, but even his voice sounded a tad uncertain.

Suddenly, like a specter rising from the shadows, a car appeared pulled over to the side of the road. A man stood there, his silhouette stark against the night, thumb raised high in the universal gesture of hitchhiking. My instincts kicked in, and I immediately felt a rush of apprehension. Under normal circumstances, I wouldn't have even considered stopping. Yet, given the isolation of our surroundings, I found myself wavering. My experiences on the road flashed through my mind—those tales of kindness turned sour, of strangers revealing their true natures.

"Yeah, right," I muttered, shaking my head. "I'm not picking up some random guy in the middle of nowhere. It's not worth the risk."

Alex, who had been staring out the window, turned to me, eyebrows raised in disbelief. "So you're just going to leave the man stranded out here? What if he really needs help?"

I didn't slow down, despite the urgency in his voice. "Come on, man. We don't even know if he's really in trouble. He could be just trying to bait us. You've seen those movies, right?"

He scoffed, crossing his arms. "This isn't a movie! It's just a guy needing a ride. You can't be serious! It's not like we're in the city—this is the middle of nowhere. Come on, let's go back."

I stared at him for a moment, weighing his words against my gut feeling. It felt like an eternity, but in reality, it was just a few seconds. Finally, I sighed, conceding to the growing sense of guilt gnawing at me. "If this guy turns out to be a murderer, I'm totally haunting you."

With a reluctant nod, I turned the car around, the engine rumbling to life once more. As we approached him again, I noticed the way his posture shifted—his shoulders straightened, and a spark of hope ignited in his eyes when he saw us coming back. It was as if he had just spotted a lighthouse in a stormy sea. I felt a strange mix of trepidation and curiosity as I pulled up beside him, the window sliding down with a slow creak.

Waving him into the car, I noticed he was probably a few years older than Alex and me. "Hey, I'm Trent. Good to meet ya," he said, a mix of relief and gratitude in his voice. "I haven't seen anyone in a while, and when you passed, I wasn't sure how much longer I was going to have to wait. Thanks for stopping, by the way. I ran out of gas back there. I'm going to have to get a tow at the next town."

"Yeah, no problem," I replied, trying to sound casual despite the growing unease in my gut.

Alex was quick to respond, ever the friendly one.

"That sucks, man. Well, we'll get you there. By the way, I'm Alex, and this is Chris."

I nodded, focusing on the road ahead, my mind racing. As they engaged in a light conversation, a flicker of movement caught my eye. Glancing to my right, I spotted a woman and a couple of kids standing just a foot into the road, their eyes fixed on the dense woods, as if something unseen beckoned them. If I hadn't been paying attention, I might have run them down. Instead, I eased the car around them, but the whole situation felt off-kilter. I couldn't shake the feeling that something was wrong, so I pulled over, determined to check on them.

The sudden lane change interrupted Trent and Alex mid-conversation. They both turned their heads, spotting the trio as I stepped out of the car. "What are you doing?" Alex called, his voice tinged with concern.

"I just want to make sure they're okay," I replied, glancing back at him. He hesitated, then shrugged, deciding to stay put.

As I walked closer, an unsettling dread settled in

my stomach. The closer I got, the more I felt a chill in the air, a sense of foreboding that made my skin prickle. Something was definitely off about this situation, but I couldn't quite put my finger on it.

Almost in unison, the woman and children turned toward me, their pale skin glimmering unnaturally in the fading light. I noticed, even from a distance, that there were no whites in their eyes—just large black pools that seemed to consume the light around them. My heart raced as they raised their hands, reaching out toward me, mouths opening in a wordless scream. A bright light flashed behind me, pulling my attention away. I turned to see two glaring headlights bearing down on us, a truck roaring down the road, and panic gripped me. "Get back in the car!" I shouted, my voice barely registering over the engine's growl.

It was too close to move; even Travis seemed frozen in shock at what was happening. The world around us felt like it had slowed down to a crawl, a surreal moment suspended in time. My heart raced, thundering in my chest like a war drum, and I could feel the cold sweat trickling down my back. I knew I was going to die. There was no alternative option. Just then, the truck seemed to pass through us, a ghostly blur that rushed headlong into the woman and her children. I gasped, my mouth agape as the scene unfolded before my eyes. All at once, the truck, the woman, and the kids were gone, as if they had never existed at all.

Travis stood beside me, his face pale as a sheet, eyes wide with disbelief. "Did you see that?" he finally managed to croak, his voice barely above a whisper, as if speaking too loudly would shatter the fragile reality we found ourselves in.

I could barely respond; my throat felt tight, constricted by the weight of what we'd just witnessed. "I… I don't know what just happened," I stammered, my mind racing to comprehend the impossible. The only thing I knew for sure was that I would need to change my pants before getting back in the car, given that fear had loosened my bladder.

As we finally stumbled back into the car, I glanced at Alex, who had been sitting quietly, his face scrunching up in confusion. "You guys are just overreacting," he said, though the way he was breathing hard and shifting in his seat told a different story. I caught his eye, and for a fleeting moment, I thought I saw a flicker of fear there.

To this day, I believe what we saw that day was a remnant of an event that had transpired at that spot long ago. A few weeks later, I found myself standing at that same intersection, clutching a wooden cross I had carved in my workshop. I wanted to give the spirits there the acknowledgment they deserved. "This is for you," I murmured softly, placing the cross carefully into the ground.

Alex, who had reluctantly accompanied me, shook his head. "I still don't think it'll make a difference," he said, his skepticism evident. "What you're describing sounds like a residual haunting, not something that can hear you."

But even as he spoke, I felt a deep conviction in my heart. "They deserve to be remembered," I replied firmly, my voice steady. "Even if we never met them in life, they shouldn't be forgotten." The wind rustled around us, and for a brief moment, I thought I could almost hear a whisper carried on the breeze, thanking me for my small act of remembrance.

HAUNTED BY A FULL MOON

CHAPTER 8

HAUNTED BY A FULL MOON

A fog rolls in over the B1249 as dusk settles, wrapping the road in a thick, eerie cloak. This winding stretch of asphalt, meandering through the East Riding of Yorkshire, is not just a thoroughfare but a canvas for tales of the supernatural and the macabre. Known for its haunted reputation, the B1249 has become an epicenter of chilling stories, spine-tingling sightings, and a dash of folklore that keeps both locals and daring travelers on edge.

The Legend of the Yorkshire Werewolf

The B1249, a winding ribbon of asphalt that slices through the desolate moors of Yorkshire, is perhaps best known for the chilling legend of the Yorkshire Werewolf—a malevolent creature that has haunted these shadowy landscapes long enough to become entrenched in local lore. Picture yourself navigating a lonely stretch of this road, where the air hangs thick with an unsettling stillness. Suddenly, from the depths of the encroaching darkness, a towering figure emerges, its glowing red eyes piercing the night like two smoldering coals. This is no mere figment of imagination; it is a nightmarish reality that has gripped the hearts of those unfortunate enough to cross paths with this spectral beast.

The first documented sighting of this creature dates back to the 1960s, when a weary lorry driver found himself inexplicably drawn to a clearing bathed in the pale light of a waning moon. There, he was confronted by an enormous, wolf-like being, standing upright and exuding an aura of dread. Its muscular body, cloaked in a thick, matted coat of dark fur, seemed to absorb the feeble light around it, rendering it a shadow among shadows. The driver's heart raced as he locked eyes with the beast; its gaze was a chilling mix of hunger and malice, a deep, primal intelligence that sent shivers cascading down his spine.

As he sped away, the echo of howling winds filled his ears, mingling with the sound of his thundering heart. The creature remained etched in his memory, a haunting specter of pure terror. Over the years, whispers of similar encounters have rippled through the community like an ominous fog, as countless witnesses recounted their own harrowing tales of the beast. Each account shared eerie similarities: the creature's unnatural speed, darting across the road with an agility that defied the laws of nature, leaving only a chilling silence in its wake. Locals often speak of the night when the air grows heavy with the scent of damp earth and decay, when the moon hangs low and full, casting long, grotesque shadows that seem to dance in anticipation. On those nights, it is said, the werewolf stirs, prowling the moors once more, hungry for the thrill of the hunt.

Tales from the Shadows

One particularly harrowing encounter unfolded on a moonless night in the 1980s, when a family found themselves navigating the desolate stretch of the

B1249. The asphalt glimmered faintly under the dim glow of their headlights, creating a thin veil of light in the oppressive darkness that enveloped the world around them. Suddenly, the driver's heart lurched as he spotted a grotesque figure lounging lazily in the middle of the road, a nightmarish silhouette against the inky backdrop of the forest.

He slammed on the brakes, the tires screeching in protest, and time seemed to stretch into infinity as the family became transfixed by the creature before them. Its body, unnaturally human in shape, rippled with muscles beneath matted fur that gleamed like shadows in the dim light. The head, however, was a chilling parody of nature—a wolfish visage, eyes glowing like embers, filled with a predatory intelligence that sent shivers racing down their spines. It stared back, unblinking, as if it were weighing the worth of the terrified family squirming within the confines of their vehicle, contemplating which one might serve as its next meal.

Then, as if summoned by the very fabric of night, it vanished into the surrounding woods, leaving behind only a whisper of its presence. Shaken to their core, the family reported the sighting to local police, but no trace of the creature was ever found, as if it had never existed at all. Such moments invite a chilling contemplation of fear itself—is it merely an overactive imagination, or is there something truly sinister lurking in the shadows, waiting patiently for the next unwitting soul to wander too close? The darkness, it seems, holds secrets that are best left undisturbed, a realm where the line between reality and nightmare blurs, and something ancient stirs.

The Howls of the Night

Adding to the supernatural lore, many locals have reported hearing blood-curdling howls echoing through the night, sending chills down their spines. The creature is said to be most active during full moons, when the night sky casts an otherworldly glow over the landscape. It is as if the moon itself awakens the beast, compelling it to roam the darkened roads. For those who live nearby, it's not just tales of a werewolf that haunt their nights but the palpable fear of the unknown that keeps them peering into the darkness.

Farmers in the area have also reported unsettling occurrences. Livestock has been found dead under mysterious circumstances, with bodies showing signs of violent attacks. Large, wolf-like tracks have been discovered near fields, further fueling speculation about the Yorkshire Werewolf's existence. Some locals even whisper of a shapeshifter—an entity that takes on human form during the day, only to transform into its monstrous guise at night. The blend of the natural and the supernatural creates an unsettling tapestry of fear and fascination.

Historical Context: A Road of Shadows and Sorrow

Historically, the B1249 runs through a region steeped in rich folklore and dark histories. Real wolves roamed the woodlands of East Riding until the 15th century, when they were hunted to extinction, leaving behind a legacy that lingers in the air. The transformation of apex predators into mere memories adds another layer of complexity to the werewolf legend. After all, if the wolves once ruled the night, could their spirits still roam, embodying the essence of what they once were?

The B1249 is not just a road; it's a passage through time, carrying with it stories of tragedy and loss. The area has witnessed its share of historical crimes, adding a grim undertone to the folklore. Some locals recount tales of mysterious disappearances, accidents, and unsolved mysteries that seem to echo through the ages. The intersection of these tragic events with the otherworldly stories of the werewolf creates a perfect storm of intrigue and dread.

Modern Sightings: The Haunting Continues

Fast forward to recent years, and the legend of the Yorkshire Werewolf remains a dark specter, whispering through the shadows of the moors. In August 2016, an encounter reported by a young woman named Jemma Waller would send icy tendrils of fear creeping down anyone's spine. She described a creature that loomed before her—a hulking beast, larger than her car, its sinewy form cloaked in matted fur that seemed to absorb the light around it. As it emerged from the gnarled underbrush, its eyes glowed with an unnatural luminescence, reflecting a haunting intelligence that sent her heart racing. The face it bore was a grotesque parody of humanity; its features twisted and elongated, a jarring fusion of canine ferocity and human sorrow.

Despite the technological advancements of modern society, the allure of the supernatural persists like a moth drawn to a flame. Paranormal investigators, armed with cameras and gadgets that beep and whir, have flocked to the area, their eyes wide with a mix of skepticism and hope. They scour the fog-swathed landscape, hoping to capture evidence of the elusive werewolf, yet, despite their fervent efforts, nothing definitive has emerged. Is it possible that this creature exists in a realm beyond scientific understanding, lurking in the spaces where reality blurs into nightmare? Or is it merely a figment of collective imagination—an echo of primal fear, fueled by age-old folklore and the restless whispers of the wind that sweep across the desolate moors? As dusk falls and shadows lengthen, the haunting continues, a chilling reminder that some legends refuse to die.

A Journey into the Unknown

For those brave enough to traverse the B1249, especially on dark, moonlit nights, the road transforms into an unsettling journey. With each bend and shadow, the anticipation of an encounter looms large. It's a peculiar blend of excitement and dread that makes the heart race faster than the speedometer. The fear of the unknown becomes a companion, whispering tales of the werewolf as tires crunch over gravel and the headlights slice through the darkness.

The B1249 is more than just a road; it is a testament to the power of storytelling, where fear and curiosity intertwine. For some, the legend of the Yorkshire Werewolf is a mere tale to share around a campfire, while for others, it is a haunting reminder of the mysteries that lie just beyond the veil of the ordinary. The road invites introspection—what is it about fear that fascinates? Why do we seek out the thrill of the unknown, even when it chills us to the bone?

The B1249's Enduring Legacy

In the heart of East Riding, the B1249 stands as a symbol of the unexplained—a place where history, legend, and the supernatural converge. The haunting tales of the Yorkshire Werewolf, combined with the eerie atmosphere that envelops the road, create a captivating narrative that continues to draw in curious souls. Whether one believes in the creature or not, the thrill of the unknown is undeniable.

As night falls and darkness blankets the B1249, the ghostly whispers of the past echo through the trees. The line between myth and reality blurs, leaving behind an unsettling allure that beckons the brave and the curious. After all, who wouldn't want to drive down a road where every shadow could hide a secret, every rustle could be the wind—or perhaps, just perhaps, a lurking werewolf?

HAUNTED A272

CHAPTER 9

HAUNTED A272

Nestled within the rolling hills of Sussex, The A272 Road meanders through picturesque landscapes that evoke pastoral charm. Yet, beneath this serene facade lies an undercurrent of eerie tales and ghostly encounters that have earned it a reputation as one of the UK's most haunted roads. As the sun dips below the horizon and twilight casts long shadows, the road transforms into a stage for the supernatural, where the past lingers like a fog that refuses to lift.

The Phantom Coach of A272

Among the many spectral inhabitants that haunt the winding lanes of A272, none is as notorious as the ghostly coach, gliding silently along the cracked asphalt, its presence a chilling whisper even on the sunniest of afternoons. Local lore, steeped in shadows and sorrow, tells of a mail coach that met a tragic fate centuries ago. Driven by reckless abandon, it careened off the road, plunging into the yawning abyss of a ravine, tragically claiming the lives of all aboard.

Witnesses recount harrowing visions of the spectral coach, drawn by four magnificent horses, their coats gleaming like polished obsidian. The driver, swathed in tattered 18th-century attire, bears an expression of sheer anxiety, his gaunt features flickering like candlelight in the dark. The air grows heavy, thick with the metallic tang of fear, especially on misty nights when the fog rolls in like a shroud, obscuring all but the faintest glimmer of headlights.

On one fateful evening in the early 20th century, a group of travelers, their laughter a fragile melody against the encroaching gloom, found themselves on this haunted stretch of road. Suddenly, as if conjured from the very depths of their fears, a shadow loomed—an imposing coach hurtling toward them, wheels churning the air into a tempest of sound. Just as they braced for an inevitable collision, the apparition dissipated into the ether, leaving behind only the echo of terror and the unsettling question of their own sanity.

For those who dare to traverse The A272, the legend of the phantom coach not only captivates the imagination, but it also beckons a deeper introspection about the nature of fear itself. What drives humanity to seek out the eerie and the unknown? Is it mere curiosity, or is there a profound longing to connect with the echoes of the past, to unearth the stories buried beneath the weight of time? Each whisper of the wind through the trees seems to carry the answer, a haunting reminder that some roads lead only to shadows, where the past and present entwine in a haunting dance.

The Mysterious Mist

As if the ghostly coach weren't enough, The A272 is also notorious for a peculiar mist that appears without warning, shrouding the road in a veil of unsettling uncertainty. Those who have driven through this ethereal fog report an inexplicable sense of unease, as if unseen eyes are watching from the shadows. Accompanied by strange lights and sounds—like the clattering of hooves or the creaking of wooden wheels—this mist adds another layer to the road's haunted reputation.

Imagine cruising down The A272, the landscape a blur of greens and browns, when suddenly the world is swallowed by a dense fog. Visibility plummets, and the comforting hum of the engine is drowned out by an eerie silence. Drivers have described moments of sheer panic, feeling an unnatural urge to swerve or brake, often resulting in near-misses or accidents. Those who are brave enough to venture into the mist sometimes catch glimpses of shadowy figures darting just out of reach, vanishing as quickly as they appear. It's enough to make one ponder: is it the mist itself that is haunted, or does it serve as a portal to a realm of the restless?

The Tramp at Buck Barn

While the phantom coach captures the imagination, the spectral figure known as the Tramp at Buck

Barn has woven itself into the very fabric of local legend, casting an eerie shadow over the busy crossroads where the A272 meets the A24. It is said that as dusk descends, a shroud of mist envelops the area, and the air grows thick with an unsettling stillness. The Tramp emerges from the swirling fog, a ghostly silhouette that seems to glide rather than walk. Draped in tattered garments that shimmer between shades of ghostly grey and murky brown, he appears almost otherworldly, an apparition from a forgotten time.

Without warning, he steps into the carriageway, ambling nonchalantly in front of speeding cars. His presence sends shivers down the spines of those behind the wheel, their hearts pounding in a frantic rhythm as they slam on their brakes, tires screeching against the asphalt. The night air fills with the acrid scent of burning rubber, merging with the palpable tension that hangs heavy like a thundercloud.

Once the initial panic subsides, the Tramp simply vanishes into the mist, leaving behind a bewildered silence punctuated only by the distant hum of traffic. Was he a guardian of the road, a spectral sentinel warning unsuspecting drivers of unseen perils lurking just beyond their headlights? Or a mischievous trickster, reveling in the chaos he sows among the living? As the questions linger like the fog that swirls around him, they invite an unsettling curiosity about the true nature of his existence—a tantalizing enigma that haunts the restless minds of those who dare to travel this haunted stretch of road. The very essence of his being seems to whisper of lost souls and forgotten tales, weaving a spine-chilling narrative that echoes long after the last car has passed.

Historical Echoes and True Crime

The A272, a serpentine ribbon of asphalt slicing through the heart of Sussex, has borne witness to a cavalcade of grim accidents, each steeped in tragedy and despair. Its weathered surface is a patchwork of memories, where the ghosts of the past linger like mist in the early morning light. Each curve and bend cradles stories of lives abruptly severed, moments steeped in terror, and the haunting whispers of lost souls that flutter through the rustling leaves of the ancient oaks lining the route.

In ages long past, this very road served as a

pilgrimage path, a sacred thread connecting the cathedral cities of Winchester and Canterbury. However, the journey was anything but pious; dense, shadowy forests loomed like sentinels, while treacherous marshlands awaited the unwary. Many travelers met their grim fates here, swallowed by the earth or lost to the dark embrace of the woods. The echoes of their journeys linger like spectral sighs on the wind, begging the question: do these restless spirits still wander, searching for solace or perhaps seeking vengeance on a world that forsook them?

As twilight descends, casting elongated shadows that dance eerily across the road, the A272 transforms, becoming a mirror reflecting humanity's deepest fears and insatiable curiosities. The air thickens with an unsettling energy, electrifying and oppressive. Stories of the phantom coach, cloaked in a shroud of swirling fog, and the mysterious Tramp at Buck Barn float through the village like secrets whispered after dark. Locals recount their encounters with these apparitions, eyes wide with a mix of dread and fascination. For them, these tales are not mere folklore; they are woven into the very fabric of the land, a haunting legacy passed down through generations, ensuring that the sorrow and mystery of the A272 will never truly fade. The road, alive with whispers and shadows, invites those brave enough to tread its paths—yet warns them to heed the echoes of its sorrowful past.

A Cautionary Tale

Despite its beauty, The A272 is approached with caution by many locals and visitors alike. The stories that circulate—of ghostly coaches, enigmatic mists, and spectral figures—serve as a reminder that the past is never truly gone. The road seems to hold its breath, waiting for the next unsuspecting traveler who dares to traverse its haunted stretches.

The intersection of tragedy and the supernatural on The A272 invites introspection about fear itself. What is it that makes a ghost story resonate so deeply? Perhaps it's the way these tales connect us to our shared humanity, revealing the fragility of life and the mysteries that lie beyond.

As the headlights of a car cut through the darkness, illuminating the winding path ahead, one can't help but wonder what lies just beyond the reach of the light. The A272 continues to beckon with its eerie charm, a reminder that in the world of the unexplained, curiosity often outweighs fear.

THE HALLOW'S HEARTACHE

CHAPTER 10

THE HALLOW'S HEARTACHE

In the heart of Long Island, nestled within the serene yet eerie West Hills region, lie two roads steeped in folklore, mystery, and the kind of spine-tingling tales that make even the bravest souls shudder. Mount Misery Road and Sweet Hollow Road have earned their ghostly reputations, drawing thrill-seekers and curious onlookers alike into their shadowy embrace. As the sun sets and the moon casts its silvery glow, these roads come alive with whispers of the past, beckoning those with a thirst for the supernatural.

A Journey into the Past

The story of Sweet Hollow Road and Mount Misery Road stretches back through the mists of time, its history entwined with the whispers of Native American tribes who roamed these lands long before the first European settlers dared to tread upon them. The earth here is thick with secrets, a tapestry of eerie tales woven into the very soil. Archaeological excavations in the 1960s unearthed remnants of ancient encampments— cracked pottery, charred bones, and the faintest traces of fires long extinguished. These artifacts reveal that this forsaken stretch of land once served as a winter hunting ground, where the chill of the air carried the scent of pine and decay. Locals speak in hushed tones of the strange soil, dark and loamy, believed to be cursed, a precursor to the haunting stories that would echo through the ages.

As European settlers ventured into this wilderness in the early 1600s, they were drawn not only by the promise of rich game and bountiful vegetation but also by an unsettling aura that clung to the land like a shroud. Mount Misery, with its shadowy groves and twisted trees, became a place of both allure and dread. Hunting parties, emboldened by ambition, would plunge into the heart of these woods, only to find themselves ensnared by lurking dangers. The air was thick with tension, and the cries of unseen creatures echoed through the underbrush, reminding them that this land was not theirs to claim. In 1635, a stone fort was hastily constructed at the intersection of Chichester Road and West Hills Road, a grim bulwark against the encroaching darkness and the malevolent spirits said to roam the night.

By the 1700s, the establishment of the West Hill School on Sweet Hollow Road added yet another layer of chilling intrigue to this already haunted landscape. The building, now weathered and crumbling, seems to loom like a specter against the dreary sky. Legend whispers of a teacher, driven to the brink of madness by the oppressive weight of the land's sorrow, who locked her students inside, their terrified screams swallowed by the dry wind. The flames that consumed the school flickered like the last desperate gasps of the trapped souls, leaving behind nothing but charred timbers. Though no documents substantiate this harrowing tale, it lingers like a ghostly echo, forever haunting the remnants of the past, casting long shadows over those who dare to wander too close.

As twilight descends upon Sweet Hollow and Mount Misery, the air becomes thick with a palpable tension. The rustling leaves seem to whisper secrets, and the wind carries the mournful cries of those who once walked these paths. The landscape, with its gnarled trees and dimly lit trails, becomes a labyrinth of unease, where every snap of a twig feels like the stirring of something ancient and restless. Nightfall transforms these roads into a realm where the living and the spectral intertwine, and the past bleeds into the present, inviting only the brave—or the foolish—to uncover the truths buried beneath layers of time and terror.

Sweet Hollow Legend

The name "Sweet Hollow" might evoke visions of serene, rolling hills blanketed with wildflowers, where the air is thick with the heady scent of blooming honeysuckle and the gentle hum of bees fills the warm afternoon. Yet, beneath this deceptive veneer of tranquility lies a chilling tapestry woven with threads of tragedy and despair, a tale that lingers like a dark cloud over the land.

In the mid-19th century, a humble honey farmer, known only to locals as Elijah, unwittingly sealed the fate of Sweet Hollow. One fateful day, as he transported his golden harvest, he stumbled, sending barrels of viscous honey cascading down the dusty road. The thick, sticky substance pooled in the crevices of the earth, seeping into the very soil and forever sweetening the hollow—an ironic twist, for sweetness here has become a harbinger of sorrow. This road, once a mere path through meadows, transformed into a thoroughfare stained by the tears of the bereaved.

Not long after Elijah's accident, a sprawling asylum rose from the earth along Sweet Hollow Road, promising solace but delivering only nightmares. The grand structure, with its cold stone walls and towering spires, loomed ominously against the horizon, casting a long shadow over the surrounding fields. Inside, the air was thick with despair, and the wails of the lost echoed through its dimly lit corridors, a cacophony of anguish that seemed to awaken the very walls themselves. Then, one fateful night, a fire ignited, consuming the building and trapping patients and caregivers in its merciless grip. The flames danced wildly, illuminating the night sky with a hellish glow, while the anguished screams of those caught within mingled with the crackling of the inferno—a symphony of death that would haunt the hollow forever.

Years passed, and the asylum was rebuilt, but the specter of tragedy was relentless. It was not long before the flames returned, allegedly sparked by a heartbroken woman named Mary. Her sorrowful tale has become a ghostly legend whispered among the locals. Dressed in a tattered gown, Mary wanders the desolate road, her face a mask of anguish, searching tirelessly for her lost love. Her ghostly figure glides through the trees, illuminated by the pale moonlight, leaving a trail of sorrow in her wake. As she moves, the air grows colder, and the sweet scent of honey turns acrid, as if the very essence of her grief has tainted the land.

Travelers who dare to walk Sweet Hollow Road at dusk report an unsettling stillness, broken only by the soft rustle of leaves and the distant echo of a mournful cry. The shadows grow long, and whispers of Mary's name seem to float on the breeze, wrapping around the hearts of those who tread too close to her tragic tale. Sweet Hollow is a place where sweetness has turned to bitterness, where love and loss intertwine, leaving behind an unsettling reminder that some legends are better left undisturbed. The hollow, while picturesque in daylight, transforms into a realm of shadows and sorrow at night, forever haunted by the echoes of its past.

Haunting Tales Unfold

As dusk descends, a shroud of darkness envelops Mount Misery and Sweet Hollow Road, where shadows dance and the air thickens with the weight of untold stories. The Sweet Hollow Road Bridge looms ominously, a skeletal structure cloaked in a veil of despair. Its rusted girders creak under the weight of history, whispering tales of sorrow to those who dare to listen. In the 1970s, tragedy struck here, when a group of teenagers, lost to the depths of despair, chose this forlorn spot to end their lives. Their anguished cries seem to echo through the fog-laden air, leaving behind a spectral presence that lingers like a bitter chill.

Drivers traversing the bridge are forewarned: honk three times as a desperate plea, and perhaps, just perhaps, you might glimpse the sorrowful figures hanging just above, suspended in a timeless purgatory. Their translucent forms sway gently in the night breeze, their faces twisted in eternal anguish, reflecting the agony of the choices they made. Less fortunate travelers claim to have seen them leap into the path of unsuspecting vehicles, their ghostly forms barely visible until it is too late, a chilling reminder of their suffering and the lives they left behind.

Yet, the chilling atmosphere of Sweet Hollow Road is not solely defined by this haunted bridge. A spectral police officer is rumored to patrol the winding paths, his presence both unsettling and unnerving. He appears out of the darkness, an embodiment of authority, but when he turns, the truth becomes horrifyingly clear: the back of his head is a gaping void, a gruesome reminder of the violent end he met during a chaotic traffic stop. His hollow gaze pierces the night, seeking out those who traverse his domain, forever bound to the scene of his death, a tragic guardian of the road's dark secrets.

Compounding the eerie legends is the infamous black dog that roams the periphery of these haunted grounds. Described in hushed tones, this spectral hound is said to possess eyes like glowing embers, burning with a feral intensity that chills the soul. It prowls the underbrush and the edges of the road, a harbinger of death whose mere presence sends shivers racing down the spines of those who catch a fleeting glimpse. To witness this ominous beast is to receive a dreadful omen—an unspoken warning that the road holds secrets that are best left buried, secrets that can claw their way back to the surface, dragging with them the weight of sorrow and despair.

As the night deepens, the legends of Mount Misery and Sweet Hollow Road intertwine with the fog, each tale a thread in the tapestry of darkness that cloaks this forsaken place. The air becomes thick with an unshakable sense of dread, a palpable reminder of the lives lost and the restless spirits that roam, forever entwined with the shadows that stretch across the asphalt. The road, once a simple pathway, transforms into a haunting journey through the echoes of the past, where every turn holds the potential for an encounter with the unknown, and every mile is steeped in the sorrow of those who came before.

The Intersection of Crime and the Supernatural

As if the ghostly tales themselves were not enough to chill the soul, the intersection of tragedy and true crime casts a sinister shadow over these forlorn roads. The area is steeped in horrific events, a grim ledger of ambushes that claimed the lives of early settlers, their anguished cries echoing through the thick, damp fog that clings to the trees like a shroud. Modern-day crimes, too, have etched their dark legacy into the fabric of this landscape, whispering through the rustling leaves and winding paths like a mournful wind.

At the heart of this spectral narrative stands the Peace and Plenty Inn, once a bustling haven along Sweet Hollow Road. Its walls, now crumbling and cloaked in ivy, were once alive with laughter and the promise of healing waters that flowed as if blessed by the very earth itself. In the late 1890s, this miraculous elixir was bottled and dispatched to weary soldiers returning from the blood-soaked battfields of the Spanish-American War—an emblem of hope, yet tainted by the inn's tragic past. The air around the inn is thick with an unsettling duality; the cheerful clinking of glasses now replaced by an eerie silence that seems to pulsate with the weight of lost souls. Shadows dance along the edges of the inn, casting fleeting glimpses of figures long gone, their spectral forms drifting through the remnants of what was once a sanctuary. Visitors often find themselves ensnared in a chilling embrace of curiosity and dread, pondering whether the spirits of the past linger here, forever seeking solace or perhaps, in their sorrow, craving revenge against a world that has long forgotten their pain. The roads twist like serpents, leading one deeper into the unsettling unknown, where every step might awaken the restless spirits that haunt this forsaken place.

Cultural Context

To grasp the haunted legacy of Mount Misery and Sweet Hollow Road, one must delve deep into the cultural tapestry of the region, a fabric woven with threads of both beauty and darkness. Long Island, with its hauntingly serene landscapes and tumultuous history, serves as a backdrop steeped in Native American lore and colonial strife. Here, the very earth seems to pulse with the echoes of ancient rituals and whispered grievances, where the past lingers like an unwelcome specter.

The roads twist and curl through the West Hills County Park, a lush expanse of nature that conceals its own sinister secrets. The narrow pathways, often shrouded in a dense canopy of towering trees, weave through the underbrush like fingers reaching into the unknown. Sunlight struggles to pierce the thick foliage, casting eerie shadows that stretch and contort across the ground, as if the very landscape is alive with restless spirits.

Each turn reveals a new tableau of unsettling beauty: gnarled roots snake out from the earth like skeletal fingers, while the air is thick with the musty scent of damp leaves and decay. The trees, ancient sentinels, seem to whisper forgotten tales as the wind weaves through their branches, carrying with it an unsettling chorus of sighs and murmurs. Visitors are drawn to this intoxicating blend of allure and dread, their hearts racing with both excitement and trepidation. Here, in this enchanted yet menacing realm, the past and present collide, leaving an indelible mark on all who dare to tread these haunted paths. Shadows flicker in the periphery of vision, and the very ambiance throbs with a sense of anticipation, as if the woods themselves are watching, waiting for something—or someone—to reveal their darkest truths.

The Allure of the Unknown

As night descends upon Mount Misery Road and Sweet Hollow Road, the air thickens with an otherworldly energy. The ghosts of lost souls linger, weaving their stories into the fabric of the land. The roads, while seemingly ordinary in daylight, transform into corridors of the unknown after sunset, inviting the bravest and most curious to explore their mysteries.

Whether it's the tragic tale of Mary searching for her lost love or the spectral officer who never leaves his post, these roads captivate the imagination and remind us that the past is never truly buried. They serve as a reminder of the power of legend and lore, where every twist and turn may reveal a shadowy figure or a whisper from the beyond.

So, as you contemplate a visit to this haunted locale, remember to tread lightly. The spirits of Mount Misery and Sweet Hollow Road are always watching. They exist in a realm where fear meets curiosity, and for those willing to embrace the unknown, the adventure is sure to be both spine-chilling and exhilarating. Just be careful not to bring any ghosts back home with you. After all, they might find the journey to be just as intriguing as you do.

In a world where the line between reality and the supernatural blurs, Mount Misery and Sweet Hollow Road stand as a testament to the stories that haunt our collective imagination. The allure of the unknown is a powerful force, and it's this very force that continues to draw people to these fabled roads, where every legend has a grain of truth, and every shadow might just be a ghost waiting to unveil its tale.

THE SECRETS OF A21

CHAPTER II

THE SECRETS OF A21

As dusk settles over the A21 Sevenoaks Bypass, the air thickens with an unshakeable tension, setting the perfect stage for a tapestry of eerie tales and ghostly encounters. This road, a vital artery connecting London to the idyllic southeastern coast, is not only infamous for its heavy traffic but also for its haunted reputation. With each passing car, stories of the supernatural swirl, whispering secrets of the past that seem to linger like fog on the asphalt.

The Enigmatic Disappearances

The A21 is shrouded in an unsettling aura, infamous for its strange phenomena—most notably, the nightmarish vanishing of the road itself. Drivers navigating this dual carriageway often find themselves ensnared in an inexplicable labyrinth of asphalt and dread. One moment, the highway stretches out before them like a sunlit ribbon; the next, it distorts into an illusory path that veers ominously into oncoming traffic, as if mocking the very laws of nature. This haunting phenomenon is particularly concentrated at the sinister junction of the new bypass and the dilapidated remains of Old Gracious Lane, where shadows seem to dance and linger, whispering secrets lost to time.

Local lore weaves a chilling narrative around this bizarre occurrence, suggesting that it is the vengeful spirit of Gracious Lane itself—once a tranquil, tree-lined path, now severed and forgotten by the relentless march of progress. It is said that the spirit, with its grief twisted into fury, seeks to reclaim what was lost, ensnaring unsuspecting motorists and leading them astray as a form of spectral justice. On nights when the fog rolls in thick, those who traverse this cursed stretch report a chilling drop in temperature, accompanied by the sound of mournful whispers carried on the wind.

An unsettling number of fatal head-on collisions have been attributed to this ghostly trickery, raising the harrowing question: is the road cursed, or is it merely a manifestation of our deepest fears, a reflection of the dread that lurks just beneath the surface of our collective consciousness? As headlights flicker and fade, it becomes clear that the A21 is more than just a road; it is a portal to the unknown, where the boundaries between reality and the spectral blur, leaving behind an echo of despair that clings to the air like the scent of decay.

The White-Haired Woman

Among the spectral denizens of the A21, none is more chilling than the enigmatic figure of the old woman with hair as white as freshly fallen snow. Her fawn coat, tattered and stained with the shadows of forgotten memories, flutters in the wind like the wings of a moth caught in a darkened room. As dusk descends, she reportedly materializes before unsuspecting vehicles, her presence a sudden jolt that sends drivers slamming on their brakes, hearts pounding in their chests like the relentless beat of a war drum.

In a bizarre twist of fate, motorists traveling in both

directions have claimed to knock her down simultaneously—only to find no trace of her ethereal form on the asphalt, just the lingering chill of something otherworldly. Her spectral visage, serene yet sorrowful, stirs an unsettling mix of dread and fascination, drawing the gaze of onlookers even as they fight the instinct to look away.

Whispers in the night suggest she is the restless spirit of a woman who met her tragic end in these very woods in 1959, her life cruelly snuffed out by the very road she now haunts. As her ghostly figure flickers in and out of existence, a shroud of mist enveloping her like a second skin, one can't help but ponder the nature of fear itself: Is it merely an echo of her profound sorrow, or a stark reminder of the fragility of life? Each encounter leaves an indelible mark on the soul, a haunting question echoing in the silence: Who truly walks this road, the living or the dead? The air tingles with an icy dread, as if the road itself remembers her, a silent witness to the tragedy that unfolded and the spirits that linger, forever entwined with the shadows of the past.

The Running Man: A Ghost on the Run

Perhaps the most notorious specter haunting the A21 is the Running Man, a shadowy figure woven into the fabric of local legend. Cloaked in darkness, this elusive ghost is often glimpsed near Sevenoaks, where he darts across the road with an unnatural speed, provoking a visceral panic in unsuspecting drivers. The tales surrounding the Running Man are as diverse as the weary travelers who recount them; some believe he is the restless spirit of a fugitive, forever fleeing the consequences of his past, while others whisper that he was a victim of a hit-and-run, eternally condemned to relive the moment of his tragic demise—a phantom trapped in a relentless cycle of horror.

One particularly harrowing account from the 1980s recounts a family journeying home late at night along the desolate stretch of road. As they navigated the winding path shrouded in fog, the figure suddenly materialized from the depths of night, a fleeting silhouette that seemed to float rather than run. The driver, heart racing, swerved violently to avoid this specter, sending their car spiraling into a ditch with a bone-jarring thud. When they finally stumbled from the wreckage, adrenaline coursing through their veins, the air grew thick with an unsettling silence. The only sounds were the echoes of their frightened breaths and the rustling of leaves, as if the very night itself held its breath. As they frantically scanned the darkness, the chilling realization settled over them like a heavy fog: they were not alone. The Running Man had vanished, leaving behind nothing but an oppressive stillness and the lingering dread of what might still lurk in the shadows, a timeless harbinger of misfortune on the haunted A21.

Ghostly Fogs and Sudden Drops in Temperature

The A21 is not just haunted by apparitions; it is also a stage for inexplicable natural phenomena. Drivers have reported sudden drops in temperature, even on balmy evenings, as if the spirits of the road are drawing close. Alongside the chilling air, strange fogs often materialize without warning, enveloping the road in an otherworldly shroud. These fogs are not mere weather patterns; they carry a palpable sense of dread, as if unseen eyes are watching from the shadows.

As the fog creeps in, it brings with it the unsettling sensation of being observed—a classic hallmark of a haunted location. Some drivers even claim to have glimpsed ghostly figures emerging from the mist, adding to the already thick atmosphere of unease. The intersection of these eerie elements creates a perfect storm of fear and intrigue, drawing thrill-seekers and ghost hunters alike to the A21.

True Crime and Tragedy

To truly grasp the haunted legacy of the A21, one must plunge into its shadowy historical depths. This winding road, cloaked in mist and mystery, has borne witness to a staggering number of accidents and tragedies, each imbedding an additional layer of sorrow into its already macabre reputation. As twilight descends, the air grows thick with an unsettling silence, broken only by the distant wail of sirens—an eerie reminder of lives abruptly extinguished. The intersection of true crime and the supernatural weaves a chilling narrative that lingers in the minds of those who dare to traverse its length.

The A21 has long been a graveyard for dreams, a silent witness to fatal collisions that haunt its asphalt. Some of these tragedies remain shrouded in an impenetrable fog of mystery, their details lost to time, yet their impact echoes through the decades. Locals speak in hushed tones of the restless spirits that are said to roam the edges of this cursed thoroughfare. On moonless nights, drivers recount tales of flickering lights and shadowy figures darting across the road, their forms blurring in and out of focus like whispers in the dark. Could it be that these apparitions are the souls of those who met untimely ends here, forever trapped in a liminal space between the living and the dead?

The road itself seems to breathe a heavy sigh, as if lamenting the countless lives it has consumed. Each bend and curve bears the weight of sorrow, the asphalt soaked in the blood of the unfortunate. The scent of rain-soaked earth mingles with something more acrid, a metallic tang that lingers in the air—perhaps the remnants of anguish that refuse to dissipate. As dusk falls, the landscape transforms; gnarled trees loom, their twisted branches reaching out like skeletal fingers yearning for the warmth of life.

Drivers often find themselves gripped by an overwhelming sense of dread, a cold shiver creeping down their spines as they navigate this haunted stretch. The line between reality and the supernatural blurs into an indistinguishable haze, leaving one to wonder whether the A21 is more than just a road; it is a repository of lost lives and untold stories, echoing their sorrow through ghostly encounters that chill the very marrow of one's bones. Those who dare to tread its path may find themselves not only confronting the shadows of the past but also becoming unwitting participants in a haunting narrative that refuses to be forgotten.

The Cultural Context of Fear

The tales surrounding the A21 Sevenoaks Bypass evoke a sense of introspection about the nature of fear itself. What compels individuals to seek out the unknown? Is it curiosity, a thrill-seeking impulse, or a deeper desire to confront the specters of mortality? The allure of the supernatural often lies in the questions it raises about life and death, inviting individuals to explore the boundaries of their own understanding.

As drivers navigate the A21, the question lingers: is it the ghostly figures or the road itself that is truly haunted? Each encounter leaves an indelible mark on those who experience it, shaping their perceptions of fear and the unseen. The stories shared among locals serve as a communal exploration of the unknown, a reminder that the past is never truly gone, but rather exists in the echoes of our experiences.

A Road Best Taken with Caution

For those brave enough to traverse the A21, especially under the cover of night, the tales of the Running Man, the white-haired woman, and the vanishing road loom large in their minds. Each shadow becomes a potential specter, each turn a possible encounter with the unknown. Whether these stories are mere figments of imagination or genuine hauntings, they add a layer of excitement to the journey, transforming a simple drive into an adventure steeped in history and mystery.

As the A21 winds its way through the Kent countryside, it serves as a reminder that some roads hold more than just asphalt and gravel; they carry the weight of history, tragedy, and the unexplained. With each mile, the A21 Sevenoaks Bypass beckons the curious and the brave, inviting them to explore its dark corners and uncover the secrets that lie just beneath the surface.

In the end, whether one believes in ghosts or chalks it all up to overactive imaginations, the A21 remains a captivating blend of the eerie and the intriguing—a road where the past and present collide in a spectral dance that continues to haunt the living. So, for those willing to brave the journey, it's wise to keep an open mind and perhaps a flashlight—just in case the Running Man decides to make an appearance.

EERIE ECHOES OF A229

CHAPTER 12

EERIE ECHOES OF A229

As dusk descends over the ancient landscape of Kent, the A229 Road stretches like a winding ribbon through history, a thoroughfare that has borne witness to countless stories, both mundane and mysterious. This road, particularly the notorious stretch known as Blue Bell Hill, is often heralded as one of the most haunted roads in the UK. It's a place where the past refuses to stay buried, and where echoes of sorrow and mystery linger in the air, waiting to ensnare the unsuspecting traveler.

Imagine driving along the A229 as fog rolls in, cloaking the world in a shroud of gray. The headlights cut through the mist, illuminating the asphalt that has borne the weight of centuries. It's in this eerie atmosphere that tales of ghostly encounters and tragic histories come to life, offering a blend of spine-tingling intrigue and a touch of grim humor that is almost comforting—like a ghost story told around a campfire.

The Phantom Maid of the A229

Among the most chilling apparitions haunting the A229 is the spectral figure of a maid, known simply as the "phantom woman." Enveloped in an aura of sorrow, she darts across the road like a wisp of smoke, her presence sending shivers down the spines of unsuspecting drivers who slam on their brakes, hearts pounding, only to watch in horror as she dissolves into thin air, leaving nothing but an unsettling silence in her wake.

Witnesses paint a vivid picture of her: a young woman clad in tattered, old-fashioned clothing that flutters like the ghostly remnants of a bygone era. Her face, pale as moonlight, wears an expression steeped in melancholic longing, eyes glistening with unshed tears that speak of a tragic tale untold.

The legend whispers of her tragic fate, a heartbreaking story from many decades past when she met her demise while crossing the road late one fateful night after finishing her duties at a nearby manor house. The air thick with an eerie stillness, she tread softly upon the asphalt, unaware of the catastrophe that awaited her. Her spirit, forever restless and aggrieved, remains tethered to the spot where her life was so cruelly snatched away, a haunting reminder of life's fragility and the unpredictable twists of fate.

On a particularly fog-drenched night in the 1960s, a lorry driver, his breath visible in the chilling air, swerved violently to avoid what he believed to be the woman standing ghostlike in the road. Heart racing, he pulled over, the oppressive fog swirling around him like a living entity, only to find the road starkly empty, the silence punctuated by the distant howl of the wind. Shaken to his core, he reported the encounter to the police, only to discover he was not the first—and certainly not the last—to experience this spectral phenomenon. The tales of the phantom maid have woven themselves into the very fabric of local lore, igniting the imaginations of residents and visitors alike, a chilling reminder that the past is never truly buried, and some spirits linger, forever caught between worlds.

The Specter of Blue Bell Hill

A particularly notorious stretch of the A229, Blue Bell Hill, looms like a specter itself, steeped in an unsettling aura that transcends mere ghost stories. This road, winding through the dark embrace of shadowy trees and thick fog, has become the stage for a tragic tale that resonates through the years—a haunting that clings to its asphalt like an unshakable mist. On a fateful night in November 1965, the lives of 22-year-old Susan Browne and her companions were extinguished in a horrific accident that echoes in whispers, leaving behind not just memories, but a sorrowful essence that seems to linger in the very air.

As twilight descends and the moon casts an eerie glow, drivers navigating this cursed stretch often find themselves gripped by an inexplicable chill. They report catching sight of a lone woman in a tattered white dress, her figure flickering like a candle in the breeze, standing forlornly by the roadside, her eyes pleading for assistance. When compassionate souls stop to offer aid, she vanishes into the night like smoke, leaving only the icy touch of dread and a heart heavy with disbelief. Variations of this haunting tale ripple through the community—sometimes she leaves behind a small, delicate purse, its contents a bittersweet reminder of a life long lost. Other times, when drivers reach their destinations, they discover that their mysterious passenger had departed this world decades before.

In 1974, a local bricklayer named Maurice Goodenough burst into the Rochester Police Station, his face pale and eyes wide with terror, claiming he had struck a young girl on Blue Bell Hill. Wrapped in a frayed blanket, he had left her shivering at the roadside, only to return with help and find her vanished as if swallowed by the night itself. The police scoured the area, their flashlights cutting through the darkness, but the girl was never found, her fate sealed by the whispers of the wind. Such incidents have solidified Blue Bell Hill's reputation as one of the most haunted stretches of road in the UK, where the ghostly hitchhiker has morphed into a modern legend, a chilling reminder of the fragility of life that continues to intrigue and terrify all who dare to traverse its haunted path. Each passing car seems to draw the shadows closer, as if the road itself remembers and mourns the souls lost to its unforgiving embrace.

The Historical Context of A229

The A229 is steeped in history, tracing routes that date back to Roman times. Following the path of Roman Road No. 13, it has served as a vital link between Rochester and Hastings for centuries. The road was officially turnpiked in the 18th century, and its current designation as the A229 came in 1923. Along its winding path, it passes through the Medway Towns and Maidstone, leading travelers through a landscape rich with tales of yore.

The proximity to ancient estates and manor houses only adds to the road's haunted lore. The echoes of history seem to resonate in the very asphalt, whispering tales of love, loss, and the supernatural. As one drives along the A229, the shadows of the past linger at the edges of perception, inviting curiosity and igniting a sense of wonder.

True Crime and Tragedy

The intersection of true crime and the supernatural is particularly poignant along the A229. The tragic accidents that have occurred here are not merely statistics; they are stories of human lives cut short, leaving behind a palpable sense of grief. The fatal incident in 1965, which claimed the lives of three women, serves as a grim reminder of the fragility of existence.

As the years pass, the tales of these tragedies morph into something more—a blend of legend and reality, haunting the memories of those who traverse the road. The ghostly encounters that follow serve as a form of collective mourning, a way for the living to connect with the stories of those who came before.

The Allure of the A229

For thrill-seekers and paranormal enthusiasts, the A229 is a magnet, drawing them into its embrace of mystery and darkness. Local ghost tours and paranormal investigations have sprung up, inviting the curious to explore the road's haunted legacy. The eerie charm of the A229, coupled with its rich history, makes it a prime destination for those seeking a brush with the supernatural.

Yet, the road also serves as a reminder of the nature of fear itself. The tales of the phantom maid and the hitchhiker evoke a sense of unease, inviting introspection about what lies beyond the veil of the known. Why do we seek out such stories? Is it the thrill of the unknown, the allure of danger, or perhaps a longing to connect with something greater than ourselves?

In the end, the A229 Road stands as a testament to the intersection of history, tragedy, and the supernatural. It is a place where the past refuses to remain buried and where the stories of those who came before continue to resonate. Whether a ghostly apparition or a mere figment of imagination, the haunting tales of the A229 are woven into the very fabric of this ancient road, inviting all who dare to traverse it to ponder the mysteries that lie just beyond the shadows.

As travelers navigate the winding path, hearts pounding and minds racing, they carry with them the echoes of those who have come before, a tapestry of lives intertwined with the history of the A229. And perhaps, as the fog thickens and the night deepens, they might catch a glimpse of the spectral maid, reminding them that some stories never truly end—they simply linger, waiting for the next curious soul to uncover their secrets.

MYSTERIOUS A75

CHAPTER 13

MYSTERIOUS A75

The A75, a stretch of road in the enchanting southwest of Scotland, is an unassuming thoroughfare bustling with traffic, yet cloaked in an aura of mystery. Known colloquially as Annan Road, this notorious route has earned its stripes as one of Scotland's most haunted highways, where the veil between the living and the spectral feels unnervingly thin. As dusk falls and the headlights illuminate the winding path, the road whispers tales of ghostly encounters, unexplained phenomena, and tragic histories that linger in the air like a ghostly fog.

The Reputation of Annan Road

Annan Road is infamous not only for its breathtaking vistas but also for the sinister tales that whisper through the rustling leaves and linger in the cool evening air. As drivers navigate its winding path, an unsettling atmosphere envelops them, where every shadow seems to pulse with a life of its own. Many recount spine-tingling encounters—shadowy figures that flit across the asphalt like wraiths escaping from the grip of darkness, ethereal animals, their eyes glowing with an otherworldly light, suddenly leaping into view before vanishing as if they were mere figments of the imagination.

The deeper one travels along this fabled highway, the more the past seeps into the present. Eerie fog often rolls in, wrapping around the towering trees that loom like sentinels, their gnarled branches clawing at the sky. Whispers of long-forgotten souls drift through the air, weaving tales of sorrow and loss that tug at the edges of the mind. Each twist and turn seems to harbor echoes of tragic events—accidents, betrayals, and unfulfilled dreams—seducing the curious and the intrepid to explore its haunted legacy. The road itself becomes a living entity, breathing in the stories of its travelers, ensnaring them in its spectral embrace, daring them to uncover the chilling truths hidden in its depths. As dusk descends, the landscape transforms into a surreal tableau, where the boundary between reality and the supernatural blurs, leaving an indelible mark on those brave enough to traverse its haunted expanse.

Ghostly Animals and Shadowy Figures

Among the most spine-chilling reports are those of ghostly animals, shrouded in an unsettling mystique that lingers long after the tales are told. One of the most notorious stories hails from the shadowy roads of the 1980s, involving a weary truck driver whose heart raced as he swerved to avoid a large dog that had inexplicably darted into his path. Heart pounding with dread, he pulled over, the stillness of the night enveloping him like a damp shroud. Yet, when he stepped out of the cab, the dog had vanished, as if swallowed by the very darkness itself, leaving behind only the echo of his own breath in the chilling air. Confused and rattled, he resumed his journey, but fate had other plans. Several miles down the road, the same spectral canine reappeared, its form less like flesh and more like a shimmering mirage gliding through the very metal of his truck. The creature seemed to beckon from the void, a haunting specter that left him utterly convinced of the supernatural.

But ghostly canines are merely the beginning of this eerie tapestry. Countless drivers have reported sightings of shadowy figures lurking by the roadside, their forms vaguely human yet unnervingly indistinct, as if crafted from the very shadows that cloaked them. Dressed in tattered, old-fashioned garb that rustled softly in the night breeze, these specters hint at tragic stories woven into the fabric of time, each lingering on the highway like a restless soul tied to a forgotten past. One particularly chilling account involves a motorist who slowed down for what appeared to be a gathering of figures in the middle of the road, their outlines flickering like candle flames. As he approached, a thick fog descended, and in a breathless moment of horror, he watched the figures dissolve into nothingness, swallowed by the night like whispers lost to the wind. The highway, it seemed, was not merely a passage of asphalt and tires, but a corridor of the lost, where the boundaries of life and death blurred, leaving behind only echoes and shadows.

The Man with a Rifle

Imagine, if you will, a traveler navigating the desolate expanse of the A75 late at night, the inky blackness swallowing the world whole. The sky hangs heavy with oppressive clouds, and the moon, a mere sliver of light, casts an eerie glow on the asphalt. Suddenly, the headlights of the vehicle pierce through the darkness, illuminating a solitary figure standing by the roadside. He is a man dressed in antiquated clothing, a weathered coat that flaps like the wings of a ghost in the chill of the night, his fingers wrapped tightly around an old rifle that appears to be as much a part of him as his own shadow.

As the driver's heart races and disbelief grips his mind, the figure seems to dissolve into the very air, leaving only an unsettling silence that envelops the road like a shroud. The traveler's pulse thrums in his ears as he questions his sanity—what secrets does this specter guard? Is he a sentinel of the road, forever bound to its mysteries, or a harbinger of something far more sinister?

Phantom Sounds and Sightings

The atmosphere grows thicker, almost palpable, as the night deepens. Strange sounds creep into the silence, echoing like whispers from forgotten souls. A rustle in the underbrush sends a jolt through the traveler's spine, each crackle like the snap of fragile bones. The night breeze carries faint, disembodied voices that seem to weave a tapestry of sorrow, each whisper a lingering lament that reverberates through the darkness.

Then, there are the fleeting apparitions—a man on horseback, his silhouette framed against the dim glow of the headlights, galloping through the mist like a specter from a bygone era. A woman draped in a flowing white nightdress glides through the trees, her face obscured but her eyes shimmering with an otherworldly light. They appear as if plucked from the pages of a ghost story, tantalizingly close yet perpetually out of reach, fading back into the shadows as if they were never there.

Witnesses report a feeling of being watched, the hairs on the back of their necks prickling in response to unseen eyes. The air thickens, a heavy fog rolling in, twisting the shapes of trees into grotesque figures, their gnarled branches reaching out like skeletal hands. The road, once a mere passage through the night, transforms into a realm teeming with unseen horrors. Each sound—a whisper, a rustle, a distant, mournful wail—seems to tell a story of loss and longing, echoing through the darkness like a morbid lullaby.

What lies beyond the veil of shadow? What ancient tales are etched into the very pavement of this haunted road? Each traveler becomes a reluctant participant in a narrative woven with threads of fear and mystery, a tale that stretches back through the years, where the past and present collide in a chilling embrace.

The Lady in White by Kinmount House

Nestled in the shadowy embrace of Kinmount House, where the air grows thick with whispers of the past, there emerges a ghostly figure known as the Lady in White. She drifts along the winding highway, her presence as ephemeral as the mist that clings to the ground at twilight. Clad in a flowing gown, the fabric seems to shimmer with a silvery luminescence, catching the pale light of the moon and casting an otherworldly glow on the asphalt. As she crosses the road, her delicate feet barely disturb the gravel beneath them, gliding as if she were a specter woven from the very fabric of the night.

What draws her to this desolate stretch of highway, where shadows stretch and twist like gnarled fingers? Perhaps she is forever searching for something lost—a treasured memory, a stolen moment, or a love that slipped through her fingers like grains of sand. Each night, she returns to the old Kelhead Quarry, a haunting reminder of her unfinished business, her eyes filled with an eternal yearning, as if the very essence of her sorrow lingers in the air like a mournful song. The quarry, with its jagged edges and deep shadows, becomes a silent witness to her endless quest, echoing the cries of the heartbroken and the lost. Travelers who inadvertently catch a glimpse of her fleeting form can't help but feel an unsettling chill run down their spines, as if the air itself mourns her fate.

The Mysterious Figures of Brydekirk Junction

At Brydekirk Junction, reality begins to dissolve, merging seamlessly with the realm of the supernatural. On a fog-laden evening, a weary motorist and her young son find themselves ensnared in an encounter that defies explanation. As they pause at the junction, a bright white light suddenly envelops their car, illuminating the night with an intensity that contrasts sharply with the oppressive darkness surrounding them. The light reveals a figure standing just beyond their window, a silhouette that flickers like a candle in the wind, accompanied by an unsettling aroma of stale cigarette smoke, as though the very air has absorbed the essence of countless late-night conversations.

The figure hovers just out of reach, shrouded in an aura of both familiarity and dread, evoking a sense of recognition that is almost tangible yet frustratingly elusive. Just as quickly as it appears, the apparition vanishes, leaving behind a disorienting silence that fills the car like an unseen weight. The mother glances at her son, who stares wide-eyed, his innocence untouched by the fear that grips her heart. What secrets does this spectral entity carry, and why does it linger at this threshold between worlds? Are these figures remnants of lives once lived, yearning for acknowledgment, or are they restless souls, adrift in the currents of time, seeking solace in the forgotten corners of existence?

In the stillness that follows, the air grows thick with unanswered questions, and the tension of the moment hangs like fog in the night. As they drive away, the scent of smoke lingers, a ghostly reminder of what they've encountered, a fleeting connection to a reality that feels both frightening and profoundly human. The line between the living and the dead continues to blur, and the stories of Kinmount House and Brydekirk Junction weave together, creating a tapestry of longing, loss, and the ever-present shadow of the unknown.

The haunted tales of the A75 are intricately woven with the fabric of history. This road has been the scene of numerous tragedies, accidents, and even criminal events that have contributed to its eerie reputation. The intersection of true crime and the supernatural creates a chilling backdrop that deepens the haunting atmosphere.

The Ferguson Brothers' Terrifying Experience

In the bleak, shadow-laden hours of 1962, Derek and Norman Ferguson found themselves navigating the desolate stretch of the A75 near Kinmount, the moon hanging low and ominous in a starless sky. The landscape, cloaked in an unsettling stillness, seemed to whisper secrets of the forgotten. Suddenly, a large hen, its feathers ruffled like a spectral wraith, hurtled toward their windshield, only to evaporate into the night air just inches from impact, leaving behind an icy chill that seeped into their bones.

Heartbeats quickening, the brothers squinted into the darkness, where the silhouette of an old woman emerged, her gnarled hands waving frantically, as if caught in a tempest of despair. Her eyes, wide and hollow, seemed to pierce through the veil of night, drawing them into an abyss of unease. Behind her, a man with wild, unkempt hair appeared, his screams echoing like a banshee's wail, a sound so raw and filled with anguish it sent shivers down their spines.

Then, from the very shadows, an array of bizarre creatures materialized—wild dogs with matted fur and eyes that glowed like embers in a dying fire, phantom cats that slinked through the air with an ethereal grace, their forms flickering like candle flames. The temperature dropped sharply, and the car began to sway violently, as if caught in an unseen vortex, the engine sputtering in protest. A palpable sense of dread enveloped them, heavy and suffocating, pressing against their chests like a shroud of darkness. To this day, the brothers remain haunted by that night, the echoes of their eerie encounter reverberating through their minds like a ghostly refrain, a chilling reminder that some horrors are never truly exorcised from the soul.

Legends and Witchcraft Theories

As twilight descends upon the desolate stretches of the A75, a thick, eerie fog rolls in, shrouding the landscape in a ghostly veil. The air grows heavy with an unsettling stillness, broken only by the occasional rustle of leaves, as if the trees themselves are whispering secrets long buried. Delving deeper into the local lore, townsfolk huddle in dimly lit taverns, their voices dropping to hushed tones, weaving tales of witchcraft that send shivers down the spine.

The region is steeped in a rich tapestry of dark history, where crumbling stone cottages and shadowy woodlands speak of covens that once gathered under the full moon, their rituals echoing through the ages. They claim that the spirits of wronged witches—betrayed, accused, and burned—still roam the earth, their spectral forms flickering in and out of sight, seeking retribution or perhaps yearning to share their sorrow.

A sense of foreboding permeates the air, as if the very ground beneath the A75 is haunted by the weight of ancient grievances. The chilling atmosphere invites speculation that these restless souls linger at the fringes of reality, their whispers carried by the wind, blending with the mournful cries of the night. Each shadow that stretches across the path seems alive with their sorrow, creating a tantalizing narrative of tragedy intertwined with the supernatural, forever haunting those who dare to traverse this forsaken stretch of road. The legends persist, drawing in the curious and the brave, but also warning of the unseen forces that may still linger, waiting in the darkness.

A Road Less Traveled

The A75 is more than just a road; it is a tapestry of history, mystery, and the supernatural. The mostly single-carriageway road has undergone numerous realignments and bypasses, yet the stories remain entrenched in the collective memory of those who traverse it. Sprinkled with quaint settlements like Springholm and Crocketford, the road meanders through a landscape steeped in history, making it a captivating journey for both the curious traveler and the seasoned ghost hunter.

The Kinmount Straight

The stretch of the A75 known as the Kinmount Straight, a four-mile stretch between Carrutherstown and Annan, is particularly notorious for its ghostly happenings. The adjacent Kelhead Moss Plantation, with its dense thicket of trees, serves as a backdrop to numerous reported sightings. Drivers often find themselves gripped by an inexplicable sense of foreboding, as if the very road itself holds its breath, waiting for the next encounter with the unexplained.

The Roman Legion

Amidst the swirling mists that cloak the A75, there have been whispers of a ghostly legion, an apparition of ancient warriors that emerges from the very soil of history. As twilight descends, the air thickens with a palpable tension, and those brave enough to traverse this haunted stretch have reported chilling sightings. The spectral figures, clad in faded armor that gleams dully like tarnished silver, march steadfastly along the road, their forms shimmering and translucent. Strangely, they appear only from the knees up, their lower halves shrouded in an unsettling fog that swirls like restless spirits.

Each soldier's face is etched with a haunting solemnity, eyes hollow yet fierce, as if forever bound to a forgotten battle. The faint sound of clinking metal echoes through the air, a ghostly symphony that sends shivers down the spine, mingling with the distant rustle of dead leaves. The scent of damp earth and ancient sweat clings to the breeze, a reminder of the blood-soaked soil beneath. This spectral procession weaves through the mist, a vivid tapestry of history entwined with the ethereal, blurring the boundaries of time and reality. Witnesses often find themselves entranced, caught in the spell of a bygone era, where the echoes of war and valor linger, reminding us that some legends never truly fade away.

The Haunting Legacy of A75

The A75, or Annan Road, stands as a testament to the power of stories, both told and untold. It is a road where the past continues to haunt the present, where every shadow seems to conceal a tale waiting to be uncovered. For those who dare to traverse its path, a sense of unease lingers—a reminder that the supernatural realm may be closer than it seems.

Whether one views these phenomena as mere figments of imagination or as genuine encounters with the otherworldly, the A75 remains a hauntingly beautiful stretch of road, inviting all to explore its mysteries. The tales of ghostly apparitions, chilling encounters, and tragic histories create a rich tapestry that captivates the imagination and stirs the soul. As night descends and the headlights flicker through the darkness, the A75 beckons—an invitation to confront the unknown, to embrace the eerie, and to journey down a road where the past is never truly gone.

THE JUMPER

CHAPTER 14

THE JUMPER

A real ghostly encounter

Every town has that place where tragedy seems to rear its ugly head more than most. That one specific location where you avert your gaze and try to pretend that your eyes don't follow it out of the corner of your eye. A place where the very air feels heavy, thick with sorrow, and acknowledging it would tempt the possibility that the negative energy would somehow take notice. I always felt a chill run down my spine when I passed by, as if the bridge was a living thing, watching, waiting.

In my town, that place is the small bridge that crosses the river between the northern and southern parts of the city. I can still hear the whispers of the locals echoing in my mind. "Did you hear about the girl last summer?" someone would say, their voice low and trembling. "They found her in the river, just beneath the bridge." Each story seemed to layer on the desolation, like sediment settling on the riverbed.

There have been more than our fair share of drownings, accidents, and suicides that have occurred there over the years. Even when someone new moves in, it doesn't take long before they, themselves, speak of the bridge and the bad vibes that exist there, almost as if they were a native. "You feel it too, don't you?" my friend Claire had asked one evening as we stood at the bridge's edge, the water below swirling ominously. I nodded, unable to voice the dread that constricted my throat. "It's like the bridge knows," she whispered, her eyes wide. There's just no escaping it, I thought, as the wind seemed to carry a distant, mournful sigh.

I had never been one to believe in things like fate or curses. Even the concept of ghosts was beyond my ability to accept. All of that changed one fateful night when my girlfriend Trina, her younger sister Sylvia, and I decided to catch a late movie. As we walked back home, the evening took a turn that would haunt my dreams to this day.

The film itself had been terrible. No amount of warm, buttery popcorn or cold soda could salvage the experience. I remember turning to Trina, her brow furrowed in disappointment. "Was it really that bad?" she asked, a hint of a smile playing on her lips. I shrugged, trying to mask my own dissatisfaction. "Let's just forget it," I replied, and Sylvia chimed in, "I want ice cream! Can we stop?"

Despite our lighthearted banter, a strange feeling settled over me as we strolled through the dimly lit streets. The moon hung low, casting eerie shadows that danced along the pavement. "It's so quiet," Sylvia remarked, glancing around nervously. "Too quiet," I agreed, glancing at Trina, whose eyes flickered with unease. I tried to shake it off, but an inexplicable chill crawled up my spine, and I couldn't shake the feeling that we were being watched. Little did we know, something was lurking just beyond our sight, ready to shatter our innocence.

Trina had been my childhood crush since, well, as long as I could remember. It didn't hurt matters that she lived literally next door to me. Our backyards, separated by a rusty chain-link fence, had been the backdrop for countless summer adventures. It would have been easy to remain friends, but sometime around junior high, something changed between us. We decided that we not only liked each other, but we "like liked" each other. Those whispered confessions during sleepovers felt monumental, each word hanging in the air like a promise.

As we walked side by side, our sneakers crunching against the gravel path, I could see the old bridge looming ahead, its wooden slats darkened by age and the constant embrace of the river below. Growing up, it was impossible to ignore all the terrible things that had happened around this place. Just the year before, a boy in my class had jumped into the water on a dare, only to be trapped underwater and drown. The memory still sent chills down my spine.

"Do you think we'll ever hear his ghost?" Trina asked, her voice barely above a whisper, as if the very mention of it might summon something from the depths.

"Maybe," I replied, trying to sound nonchalant, though my heart raced. "But it's probably just an old wives' tale."

Sylvia, our mutual friend, had taken to trying to hold her breath while running across the bridge. "It would keep anything bad from happening," she insisted, her eyes wide with determination. "It's like a magic spell!"

I chuckled, shaking my head. "That's supposed to work in cemeteries, not on bridges."

"Yeah, but who knows?" Sylvia shot back, grinning. "I'm not taking any chances!"

As we approached the bridge, I noticed the way Trina's fingers brushed against mine. Just like that, the air between us thickened with unspoken words.

Sylvia, oblivious, began her ritual. "One… two… three!" she counted, her breath hitching as she took off like a shot.

I glanced at Trina, who was watching with a mixture of amusement and concern. "Think she'll make it this time?" I asked, trying to keep the mood light.

"Only if she holds her breath the whole way," Trina laughed, but her eyes darted nervously to the water below. "Come on, let's not lose her!"

With that, we raced after Sylvia, hearts pounding, the ghost stories of our childhood echoing in our minds. The bridge creaked beneath our feet, a reminder of all the secrets it held.

She was just about to take off at full sprint when I noticed a shadow dangling off the side of the bridge we were on, almost like someone was going to jump. The frigid November air wrapped around me like a vice, biting at my skin, and I shivered at the thought of someone willingly taking a plunge into the icy depths below. It was far too cold for a late-night swim, and I had to imagine this individual harbored some dark intentions. My heart raced, pounding like a drum in my ears.

"Wait!" I called out, my voice barely breaking through the wind. I grabbed Sylvia by the arm, yanking her back just in time to avoid her sprinting into the night. Her eyes widened, and she shot me a glare, confusion etched across her face.

"What are you doing, Alex?" she snapped, her voice a mix of annoyance and fear.

"I think someone's about to jump!" I said urgently, my gaze locked on the shadowy figure. I couldn't just stand there. I had to act.

"Are you serious?" Sylvia said, her tone softening as she turned to look over the edge of the bridge.

Before I could respond, I took off, my feet pounding against the cold, hard surface as I sprinted toward the figure, the chill of the metal rail biting at my palms as I reached for it. "Hey! Wait a minute, I want to talk to you!" I yelled, my voice echoing into the night, hoping to buy precious seconds.

At this point, Trina and Sylvia, having caught up, were right behind me, their expressions shifting from confusion to fear. I felt Trina's hand on my shoulder, a silent support, urging me on. Just as I was about to yell again, the unthinkable happened. The person let go, plunging out of view. My stomach dropped as I reached for the rail to look down, straining to see what had just happened. But the darkness below swallowed them whole, and I didn't see where they landed or the splash of the water where they went in. The silence that followed was deafening, a stillness that left an icy grip on my heart.

Knowing I didn't have much time, I tore down the embankment, my heart pounding in my chest like a war drum. Every step felt reckless as I raced down the steep, crumbling path, my mind darting between fear and urgency. I could barely make out the distant gurgle of the river, but I kept my focus. I couldn't afford to lose them. "Hold on!" I shouted, hoping against hope that whoever was in trouble could hear me, that they were still there.

The ground beneath my feet was slick with damp earth, and I was acutely aware of how precarious my footing was. Somehow, I managed to reach the water's edge without tumbling into the mud. I peered into the swirling depths, scanning for any sign of life. My heart sank as I realized that each passing second meant the current was pulling them further away. "Please, don't let it be too late," I muttered under my breath, desperation clawing at my throat.

Just when I was about to give in to despair, something flickered on the surface about a third of the way across. Was it a log? A piece of debris? No, it was too human-shaped. My resolve hardened. I was a strong swimmer; I could do this. Quickly, I kicked off my shoes, the soft thud of them hitting the ground barely registering in my mind as I plunged into the frigid water.

The icy shock hit me like a slap, and I gasped as the

cold seeped into my bones. Doubts flickered through my mind. What was I thinking? But the image of the floating figure spurred me on. I knew every moment counted. I pushed harder, my arms thrashing through the water, each stroke a battle against the current.

"Where are you?" I shouted, my voice almost lost in the rushing waters. The bridge loomed overhead, casting dark shadows that swallowed the last remnants of light. The water was a murky black, and with each passing moment, I felt my chances of finding them slipping away like sand through my fingers. Desperation clawed at me, but I couldn't give up. I had to believe they were still there, waiting for me to reach them before it was too late.

Then, something seemed to tug on my leg. It wasn't hard enough to pull me down, but it was insistent, like a child wanting to get my attention. I looked down, my heart racing, and came face to face with a man who I would guess was in his mid-forties. His features were sharp and haunting, his eyes wide and void of warmth. But that wasn't the strangest thing about the encounter. His skin was a whitish blue, almost translucent, as if he had emerged from the depths of the river itself. It gave off a strange sort of glow, a sickly luminescence that made the hairs on the back of my neck stand on end.

"What do you want?" I gasped, my voice barely a whisper as panic surged through me. I wanted to scream, to thrash, but fear paralyzed me.

Well, it took all of half a second before I did what any sane person would do. I panicked. I started thrashing around in the water, kicking and flailing, trying my best to look like I was being hunted by a shark. I could feel my heart hammering in my chest, drowning out all rational thought. Given that I was in a freshwater river in the middle of the continental United States, the absurdity of my situation wasn't lost on me.

I faced down current, pumping my arms as fast as I could, my legs churning the water into a frothy chaos. Each stroke felt like a desperate plea for survival, and I could almost hear my own thoughts echoing in my mind: Get out. Get out. Get out. This mantra became my lifeline, a rhythmic chant that propelled me forward as the shore loomed closer and closer.

When my feet finally touched solid ground, I felt a rush of relief. I raced out as fast as my legs could carry me, the river's cold grip releasing me just as I reached the bank. I stumbled onto the shore, panting, glancing back over my shoulder, half-expecting the glowing figure to follow. "What was that?" I muttered to myself, still trembling, the shadows of the trees seeming to whisper secrets of the river's depths.

On shore, my body shook violently, the chill from the freezing water seeping into my bones, but I knew it was the fear that truly gripped me. By the time Trina and Sylvia reached me, I had managed to gain some semblance of control over my shivering. As I looked up, I saw Trina's brow furrowed with concern, her eyes scanning my face for answers.

"What was that weird glow we saw right next to you?" she asked, her voice trembling slightly.

Her question sent my mind racing, and I found myself opening and closing my mouth like a fish out of water, desperately searching for words that seemed to elude me. How was I supposed to explain that I had seen a glowing face looking at me from the depths, without sounding like I had lost my mind? The thought of saying it out loud sent another shiver down my spine. But then I took a deep breath, steeling myself.

"I... I saw something," I finally managed to stammer. "A face. It was glowing."

Trina's eyes widened, and for a moment, the world around us faded into silence. But Sylvia, standing just a few feet away, suddenly broke down, her sobs echoing against the shoreline. "I can't believe this is happening! We need to get out of here!" she cried, her voice filled with panic.

Though it was tragic to witness her distress, I felt a wave of relief wash over me. At least we had something to focus on other than the terrifying vision I had encountered. I stepped forward, wrapping my arms around Sylvia and lifting her up, her face pressed hard against my chest.

"Just breathe, Syl," I whispered, trying to keep my voice steady as her sobs continued to shake her small frame. "We're going to be okay. Let's just get back to the road."

My heart raced as I carried her away from the water, but I could still feel the weight of the man's eyes on me, even from the shore. When I had looked into those depths, I felt his hopelessness seep into my soul, and for a moment, I understood his despair, as if the water itself was inviting me to surrender, to give in and let it take me as it had taken him.

To this day, I still have a recurring nightmare where I am in that river, cold and unforgiving. The water wraps around me like a shroud, pulling me deeper into its depths. Some nights, I manage to claw my way out, gasping for air, while others find me waking up with the taste of brackish water on my lips, my heart racing as if I were still submerged. "Not again," I'd whisper to myself, drenched in sweat. For years, I took alternative routes, avoiding that bridge like it was a cursed relic. I could still hear Trina's laughter echoing in my mind, a stark contrast to the terror that unfolded that night.

"Let's just cross quickly," she had said, her voice light and carefree. But I couldn't shake the unease.

The events of that evening were far too traumatic to relive, too vivid to forget. Eventually, Trina and I broke up, the shadow of that night looming over us like a dark cloud. Every time Sylvia saw me, her gaze would flicker with a hint of recognition, a reminder of the horror etched in my memory. I couldn't blame her; I could barely stand to look in the mirror.

That bridge left a stain on my life, a mark I could never fully wash away. Yet, somehow, I managed to be just an echo of the past, not another victim swallowed by its depths. For that, I felt a strange sense of gratitude, even if it was tinged with lingering fear. "You're lucky to be alive," I would tell myself, though luck felt like a cruel joke sometimes.

SECRETS DOWN THE DRIVE

CHAPTER 15

SECRETS DOWN THE DRIVE

A real ghostly encounter

Not every ghost story involves a house. Sure, this one does involve the area around our home, but not in the home itself. Some people might have considered this a blessing, thinking that at least the spirits didn't inhabit the place where we slept, but that wasn't necessarily the case. The air outside always felt thick with something unexplainable, a tension that prickled the back of my neck whenever dusk settled over our quiet street.

The first time we heard about the ghosts was from our son, Curtis, and his friend, Ethan, who happened to be spending the night. My husband had set up a bright blue tent in the front yard, a cozy little refuge for the boys that allowed them to bask in the thrill of camping without straying too far from the safety of home. As I watched them zip up the tent with wide eyes and excited laughter, I felt a wave of nostalgia sweep over me. I remembered my own childhood camping adventures, free and wild under the stars, but little did I know that this night would unravel into something far more sinister.

After dark, we were snuggled in bed, the soothing hum of the evening news filling the quiet room when suddenly, the boys' piercing screams erupted from outside. My heart raced, and without a moment's hesitation, I sprang from the bed, adrenaline coursing through my veins as I dashed to the front door. The sight that met me was alarming—Curtis and Ethan barreling toward me, eyes wide with terror, each boy nearly knocking me over in their frantic bid for safety.

"Mom! Mom!" Curtis gasped, his voice trembling as he stumbled into the hallway, his face pale and glistening with tears. "We heard something outside!"

"What do you mean? What happened?" I asked, my voice steady despite the panic bubbling in my chest.

"They were walking around," Ethan chimed in, his words tumbling out in a rush. "And whispering! It sounded like… like they were talking to us!"

My heart sank at the thought. I turned on the porch light, illuminating the yard in a harsh glow. "Let's go see. Maybe it was just a raccoon or something," I suggested, trying to mask my own unease. Yet, deep down, I felt a chill slither down my spine. Was it just my imagination, or did the shadows in the yard seem to shift and writhe, as if they held secrets of their own?

One thing you have to understand about our home is that we lived outside the main city limits, tucked away from the bustling noise and chaos of urban life. Our long gravel driveway snaked its way through the darkness, a lonely path bordered by wild grasses that whispered secrets as the wind rustled through them. I shivered as I thought about how far someone would have to travel just to reach our house, and the very notion sent a chill down my spine. Who would be willing to make that trek in the dead of night? The possibility itself was frightening.

I stepped outside into the cool night air, my heart still racing from the sight of the boys sprinting into the house, faces pale with fear. They had barely made it through the door when I heard their panicked voices echoing inside.

Now, clutching a flashlight, I ventured out into the darkness, determined to check the tent area for myself. The beam cut through the night, illuminating the grass and gravel of the driveway. I aimed it toward the boys' tent, which loomed like a solitary figure against the star-speckled sky, and felt a shiver run down my spine.

"Okay, boys, where do you think we need to look?" I asked, trying to keep my voice steady despite the tension in the air. Curtis and Ethan stood next to me, their eyes wide with trepidation as they scanned the shadows.

"I don't know," Curtis murmured, glancing around nervously. "Maybe over there by the trees?"

"Or maybe it was just a raccoon or something," Ethan suggested, his voice a mix of fear and bravado as he tried to shake off the lingering unease.

I nodded, shining the flashlight in the direction Curtis indicated. "Let's check it out then. We'll see if there's anything to be afraid of."

As I swept the light across the grass and the surrounding area, I found nothing—just the rustling of leaves in the breeze. "Do you see anything?" I asked, glancing back at the boys.

They exchanged uncertain looks, and I could see their fear beginning to dissipate. "Um, no," Curtis said, his voice a bit steadier now. "Maybe we were just being silly."

"Yeah, it's probably nothing," Ethan added, a nervous laugh escaping him.

I couldn't help but relax a little at their shifting moods, but a part of me still felt that thick, unsettling air pressing down around us. "Well, let's not push our luck. It's getting late, and maybe we should head back inside for now."

As we turned to walk back, the darkness seemed to linger behind us, and I couldn't shake the feeling that something was still watching.

The following morning, as the sun struggled to break through the heavy fog, my husband stepped outside to pack up the tent. I lingered in the kitchen, the remnants of last night's fear still clinging to me like a chill. "Can you check for any footprints that don't belong to the boys?" I called after him, my voice a mix of anxiety and hope. I had spent the night wrestling with the idea that perhaps the boys had simply been scared while left outside, their imaginations weaving monsters from shadows. The thought of someone actually lurking in the darkness seemed absurd, yet I couldn't shake the feeling, the nagging doubt that something wasn't quite right.

"Sure thing," he replied, his tone casual, but I noted the slight furrow in his brow. "I'll keep an eye out for animal tracks too."

Time dragged on like molasses as I washed the

breakfast dishes, my thoughts spiraling into a whirlpool of what-ifs. What if they were right? What if something had been out there? I shook my head, trying to dispel the unsettling notions that threatened to creep back in.

When he finally returned, I felt my heart drop at the expression etched on his face—it was a mix of confusion and dread. "Come here," he beckoned, urgency in his voice. I followed him upstairs, the floorboards creaking beneath my hesitant steps.

"I found something," he said, his voice lowering to a whisper as if the walls themselves might overhear. "A print. Just one."

I blinked, trying to process his words. "One print? What do you mean?"

He ran a hand through his hair, his eyes wide. "It was barefoot, and there were no other tracks. None coming or going."

My stomach twisted. "Are you serious?"

"Yes," he said, shaking his head in disbelief. "It doesn't make any sense."

A chill ran down my spine. The boys had been right after all; something had been out there, lurking just beyond the veil of our comfort. The air felt heavier now, and I knew, deep down, that we were not alone.

For days, I kept a keen eye on the outside of our home, expecting to see the person return. The boys' raucous laughter and shouting had filled the air that day, a cacophony of youthful bravado that I hoped would deter anyone from coming back. Yet, a nagging part of me wasn't so sure. Ten days later, I awoke in the dead of night, drenched in an unsettling dread that something was deeply wrong. It felt as if an unseen presence was lurking just beyond the walls of our home.

Crawling out of bed, I tiptoed across the creaking floorboards, each step echoing in the stillness of the house. I reached the window and gently pushed aside the heavy curtains, the fabric brushing against my arm like a ghostly whisper. I peered out into the darkness, straining my eyes to discern any movement. The moonlight cast eerie shadows across the yard, each flicker of light and dark igniting my imagination. That's when I saw him—a dark figure slowly making its way down the driveway.

From my vantage point, he appeared almost like a shadow come to life, swaying slightly as he walked, his movements erratic, as if he were intoxicated. My breath caught in my throat; he seemed oblivious to the world around him, his gaze fixed on the ground. I leaned closer to the window, my heart pounding like a drum in my chest. Suddenly, he stopped. I felt a chill run down my spine as his head tilted up, locking onto my window. I couldn't see his eyes, but

I could feel their weight pressing on me, heavy and insistent.

"Who are you?" I whispered to myself, the words escaping in a breathless gasp. The terrible feeling I had multiplied tenfold, squeezing my chest tighter. I can honestly say I had never been more afraid than I was in that moment, my pulse racing as if it might burst free from my ribcage.

It was probably only a few seconds that we stared at one another, but it felt like an eternity stretched between us. Time lost all meaning as my mind raced with thoughts of what he might want. And then, as quickly as he had appeared, he was gone—one moment there, the next swallowed by the night. Even the dread I had felt moments before vanished, leaving only the echo of my rapid heartbeat as I struggled to comprehend what I had just witnessed. I backed away from the window, still trembling, my mind racing with questions that had no answers.

The rational part of my mind was struggling with what I'd witnessed, and the shadows of doubt clawed at my thoughts. There was no way I had seen a person walking down our drive, only to have them vanish right before my eyes. The word "ghost" continued to flash through my mind, but the idea that I had encountered something supernatural just didn't seem possible. Ghosts weren't real, after all, right? It could have just been a trick of the light, a figment of my half-awake brain playing tricks on me. I had experienced odd sights before, moments where my mind conjured illusions from the dark, but this felt different. The physical reaction that gripped me—my heart racing, the cold sweat prickling at my skin—was far too visceral to be dismissed as mere imagination, especially when it felt as if we were locked in a gaze, if only for a fleeting second.

Feeling the weight of my anxiety, I turned to my husband, nudging him gently awake. "Honey," I whispered, my voice trembling slightly, "I think I saw someone outside."

He blinked, squinting at the dim light filtering through our curtains. "What do you mean, someone? It's the middle of the night, love." His voice was thick with sleep, and I could sense his irritation simmering beneath the surface.

"I swear, I saw a figure walking down the drive. They just... vanished." I watched his brow furrow, the skepticism etched on his face.

"A figure?" he echoed, trying to keep his tone even. "You're sure it wasn't just a shadow? It's easy to mistake things when you're still waking up."

"I know what I saw!" I insisted, my voice rising slightly, laced with desperation. "It felt so real. We were looking at each other. I could feel it!"

He sighed, clearly torn between wanting to support

me and the rationality he clung to. "Okay, but let's not jump to conclusions. It could have been a trick of the light."

In that moment, I realized that while he didn't outright tell me I was lying, the disbelief in his eyes was just as painful. I felt a chill creep up my spine, a sense of isolation settling in my chest as I lay back down, haunted by the thought that I may have witnessed something far beyond our understanding.

The next morning, with the sun barely peeking over the horizon, I gathered my courage and stepped outside to investigate the spot where I'd seen the figure. A bitterness danced down my spine, and I could feel the weight of dread settling in my stomach. I didn't think I'd find anything to support my claim, and deep down, I was hoping I wouldn't. I would have preferred to feel a bit silly than to confront the reality of what I had witnessed. But as I walked down the gravel drive, my heart sank.

In the light dirt that formed the surface, I spotted them—impressions in the earth, as if someone had been walking barefoot towards our house. I knelt down, brushing my fingers against the cool ground, tracing the delicate outlines of the prints. "No, no, this can't be real," I whispered to myself, my voice barely escaping in a trembling breath. I felt a tightening in my chest, my mind racing with questions. Had I truly seen what I thought I had?

I froze in place, the reality of the situation washing over me like a cold wave. The evidence was right in front of me, yet disbelief clung to my thoughts like a suffocating fog. I could still picture the shadowy figure standing under the gnarled oak, and the implications of its presence sent shivers through me.

Over the next year, I was woken from sleep more than a dozen times by that same chilling sight. Each encounter gripped my heart with terror, leaving me gasping for breath until it vanished into the shadows. "Jake, it's happening again!" I'd whisper urgently, my voice trembling. He would pull me close, his eyes worried but resolute. "I believe you, Sarah. We have to find a way to deal with this."

Finally, I could take it no longer. I convinced my husband that we couldn't stay in the house any longer. He understood, having seen the footprints before, and despite never witnessing the apparition himself, he had stopped questioning my claims. "Let's just move," he agreed, determination in his voice. "It's best for us."

To this day, I'm haunted by the questions that linger unanswered. Why did the ghost continue to walk down the road to our home? Was it a previous owner, or perhaps someone who had met a tragic fate on the land? I will never know. And frankly, I would rather not have to deal with a restless spirit haunting anywhere near my life again.

PLEASE REMEMBER TO LEAVE A REVIEW AFTER READING!

Check out podcasts hosted by

Eve S Evans:

The Ghost That Haunts Me

Forever Haunted Podcast

A Ghost Story

A Truly Haunted Podcast

True Whispers True Crime

Bone Chilling Tales To Keep You Awake

About the Author

Since my first publication to the present day in 2023, I have gained a wealth of knowledge about life and my exploration of the paranormal. My journey started several years ago when I lived in various haunted houses. However, it was one particular house that left me feeling drained and exhausted. Desperate for answers, I embarked on a mission to interview numerous individuals who have also experienced hauntings, regardless of their profession or background.

But what have I learned from this journey so far? I'm uncertain if I'll ever obtain the answers I seek in this lifetime. Nonetheless, I'm determined to persist in my pursuit of knowledge by conducting interviews and engaging in ghost hunting activities. I'm committed to uncovering as many answers as possible before I too become a ghost.

This year, I have a number of books scheduled for release and I am widely recognized for my compilations of "real ghost stories". However, I have decided to challenge myself by writing mostly fictional works centered around haunted houses. If you're interested in reading one of my anthologies, I recommend starting with "True Ghost Stories of First Responders", where I interview police officers, firefighters, 911 dispatchers, and other professionals who share their eeriest calls that could be considered "ghostly".

In addition, I am looking forward to publishing my paranormal memoir this year. I aspire to reveal my personal journey and experiences to readers. Until then, I want to reassure those who may be fearful or feel like they are experiencing inexplicable phenomena in their homes that they are not alone. I have been there too, and I know it can be overwhelming.

If you need someone to talk to about what you're experiencing but don't know where to turn, you can message me on Instagram or Facebook.

Acknowledgments

I would like to express my heartfelt gratitude to my children for their unwavering support, encouragement, and enthusiasm throughout the writing process. Their constant motivation and excitement for my work have been a driving force in completing each book.

A special thank you goes out to my dear friend Ryan, whose invaluable assistance and support have been instrumental in my writing journey.
I extend my sincere appreciation to my dedicated editor, who continues to shine like a rock star with their expertise and guidance.

Last but certainly not least, I am immensely grateful to all my readers who eagerly devour each of my spooky books and return for more. Your enthusiasm and loyalty fuel my passion for the paranormal genre, and I owe my continued writing journey to your unwavering support. Thank you for keeping the magic alive.

Printed in Dunstable, United Kingdom